# BFI Film Classics

W0246805

The BFI Film Classics series introduces, interprets and celebrates landmarks of world cinema. Each volume offers an argument for the film's 'classic' status, together with discussion of its production and reception history, its place within a genre or national cinema, an account of its technical and aesthetic importance, and in many cases, the author's personal response to the film.

For a full list of titles in the series, please visit
https://www.bloomsbury.com/uk/series/bfi-film-classics/

This book is dedicated with love to my family, past and present

לדור ודור

*L'dor v'dor*

From generation to generation

# Hester Street

Julia Wagner

THE BRITISH FILM INSTITUTE
Bloomsbury Publishing Plc, 50 Bedford Square, London, WC1B 3DP, UK
Bloomsbury Publishing Inc, 1385 Broadway, New York, NY 10018, USA
Bloomsbury Publishing Ireland, 29 Earlsfort Terrace, Dublin 2, D02 AY28, Ireland

BLOOMSBURY is a trademark of Bloomsbury Publishing Plc

First published in Great Britain 2025 by Bloomsbury on behalf of the
British Film Institute, 21 Stephen Street, London, W1T 1LN
www.bfi.org.uk

The BFI is a cultural charity, a National Lottery distributor, and the UK's lead organisation for film
and the moving image. We believe society needs stories. Film, television and the moving image
bring them to life, helping us to connect and understand each other better. We share the stories
of yesterday, search for the stories of today, and shape the stories of tomorrow.

Cover artwork: © Matthew Richardson
Series cover design: Louise Dugdale
Series text design: Ketchup/SE14
Images from *Hester Street* (Joan Micklin Silver, 1974), Midwest Film Productions; *Crossing Delancey*
(Joan Micklin Silver, 1988), Warner Bros.
Film stills courtesy BFI National Archive

A catalogue record for this book is available from the British Library.

A catalog record for this book is available from the Library of Congress.

ISBN:    PB:    978-1-8390-2806-9
         ePDF:  978-1-8390-2808-3
         ePUB:  978-1-8390-2807-6

Printed and bound in India

For product safety related questions contact productsafety@bloomsbury.com.

To find out more about our authors and books visit www.bloomsbury.com
and sign up for our newsletters.

# Contents

# Acknowledgments

I want to thank the publishing team who made this book possible with their expertise and enthusiasm, especially Rebecca Barden, Rex Cleaver and Sophie Contento.

Thank you Stuart Wurtzel, Ira Deutchman, Gerard Schwarz, Mark Balsam, Tim Lanza and Roberta Morris Purdee for generously giving time to share knowledge and memories. I am grateful to the staff at the BFI Reuben Library, Emily Wittenberg at the AFI and Jennifer Garza at the Nebraska Jewish Historical Society for their assistance with archive research.

Thanks to my parents Isabel and Tony for their love and encouragement. To Adam, Joseph, Miri and Bonnie, thank you for being wonderfully supportive of me throughout this project.

# Introduction

*Hester Street* (1975) is a landmark of American cinema. Filmed in black and white, and with a largely Yiddish script, Joan Micklin Silver's debut feature represents the world according to Gitl (Carol Kane), a poor, young, Jewish immigrant from the Russian Empire to New York, in 1896. When Gitl and Jake (Steven Keats), her already-assimilated husband, are reunited in America, they discover they now have little in common. Gitl negotiates conflicting ways of life, driving a story of opportunity, independence and strength of mind.

Adapting a novella by Abraham Cahan (*Yekl*, 1896), Micklin Silver shifted the perspective to the female protagonist, exploring themes of identity and assimilation. Despite scepticism from potential financial backers, *Hester Street* proved to be an instant hit with audiences and was well received by critics, leading to an award nomination from the Writers Guild of America, and an Academy Award nomination for Carol Kane. In 2011, *Hester Street* was selected for inclusion in the American National Film Registry.

The box-office profits for *Hester Street* were enough to finance Micklin Silver's next film, *Between the Lines* (1977). She went on to direct films for television and cinema throughout her long career, including *Bernice Bobs Her Hair* (1976), *Chilly Scenes of Winter* (1982, first released as *Head Over Heels* in 1979), *Crossing Delancey* (1988) and *A Fish in the Bathtub* (1998).

Despite Micklin Silver's success, this is the first book to focus exclusively on one of her films, or on her career. Though studied, discussed and screened, *Hester Street* is not yet matched by appreciation in print, and in two key areas of study in particular: close film analysis, especially from a feminist perspective, and responses to its Jewish content. This book brings together these perspectives to offer a deeper exploration of the film. Ultimately, my objectives match the aims of Micklin Silver when making *Hester Street*: to increase understanding of diverse cultures, and to give voice to the experiences of Jewish women.

*Hester Street* is unusual in many respects and it does not fit straightforwardly into one genre: it is distinctive for its cinematography, language, focus on Orthodox Jewish people, being written and directed by a woman, and produced and distributed independently. These factors may explain why the film has not received deeper study to date, as it seems to have fallen in the gaps between disciplinary divides. *Hester Street* has received some attention in studies of American independent film-making in the 1970s, and in the history of Jewish film-makers. But even in these areas, Micklin Silver's achievements tend to be minimised and sometimes omitted entirely.

From an audience perspective, *Hester Street* is a well-loved, memorable film that has been screened widely and regularly since its initial release. The story of the struggles of immigration, shown from a woman's point of view, has sustained public appeal. And yet, before the release of *Hester Street* in 1975, several film industry producers and distributors told Micklin Silver that its explicitly Jewish content would not be popular enough to make the film commercially viable. These warnings were proved wrong by the film's success and longevity. Today, *Hester Street* draws renewed interest because of the very factors that make it unusual. Recent years have witnessed a resurgence in Yiddish culture (Pasikowska-Schnass 2022) and greater efforts to shed light on historic films made by women, leading to screenings of Micklin Silver's films.

In these pages, I aim to illuminate the world of Jewish immigrants to New York in the 1890s. I hope to increase understanding of the community depicted in *Hester Street* and to show why Gitl, and Joan Micklin Silver, deserve to be recognised as pioneers in the history of cinema.

# 1 One More Problem We DO Need: Getting *Hester Street* Off the Ground

I had such blatantly sexist things said to me by studio executives when I started, the most outstanding of which was, 'Feature films are very expensive to mount and to distribute, and woman directors are one more problem we don't need.' (Micklin Silver 1979: 6)

*Hester Street* was shaped by the cultural environment in which Joan Micklin Silver was working. The stark insult about women directors articulates the prejudice that confronted women in the film industry. It exposes the commercial heart of the business, suggests the caution taken in investment, expresses the rarity of women directors and insinuates that all constitute one problem. If women were thought to be one problem, the nature of Jewish representation in *Hester Street* was another. Through examining the state of American film production, the position of women in the industry and Jewish film-making culture in the 1970s, we can better understand why producers considered *Hester Street* to be a risk, and appreciate Micklin Silver's part in changing the scene.

Joan Micklin was born in 1935 in Omaha, Nebraska, to Russian Jewish immigrant parents. In 1956, she graduated from Sarah Lawrence College, New York, and soon afterwards married Raphael (Ray) Silver, later having three daughters. Raphael's father was a prominent, Lithuania-born rabbi living in Cleveland, Ohio, where Joan, Raphael and their children lived until 1967. Joan worked as a music teacher, and wrote and directed plays. In 1967, they moved to New York. Joan wrote for the *Village Voice* before scriptwriting educational films for Encyclopaedia Britannica Films and the Learning Corporation of America, where she developed a successful professional partnership with producer Linda Gottlieb.

The pair worked together on three short films: *The Immigrant Experience: The Long Long Journey* (1972), *The Fur Coat Club* (1973) and *The Case of the Elevator Duck* (1974). Micklin Silver wanted to progress to directing feature films, taking what seemed to be a natural step in a career trajectory that she witnessed her male contemporaries achieve.

Micklin Silver's determination to exercise creative control as a director was spurred by her experience as a screenwriter. In 1972, her screenplay of *Limbo*, a story of wives of American prisoners of war and men missing in action in Vietnam, was sold to Universal. Micklin Silver and director Mark Robson disagreed over script revisions and she was replaced as scriptwriter by James Bridges, a decision which 'devastated' Micklin Silver, who called it a 'gruesome' and 'painful' experience. Despite their differences of opinion, Robson invited Micklin Silver to observe the set while filming took place. The process was formative:

It made me decide that I wanted to direct films right away and not wait as long as I had planned to. I'd had this wonderful plan: I was going to write screenplays, work with all the great directors, and at the perfect moment, step out and direct my own [...] But after *Limbo*, I went back to the educational film company, and asked them if I could direct a short film as well as write it and they let me. (Micklin Silver 1979: 47)

However, when she later started work on her feature-length adaptation of *Hester Street*, she encountered difficulty in raising funds and bringing producers on board.

Linda Gottlieb (who went on to produce *Dirty Dancing* in 1987) turned down Micklin Silver's proposal to work on *Hester Street*, as the producer could not see its potential (Morris Purdee 2024). Micklin Silver then sought other partners and options for funding, but discovered that nobody would take a risk on her as a female film director, particularly in a period when Hollywood and mainstream film producers were under increasing financial pressure.

By the 1970s, the studio system which had previously sustained Hollywood's success was losing its grip on the industry. The Golden Age of Hollywood, which had started in the 1930s, was in decline as the vertical integration model through which studios produced and distributed films was collapsing. Financial recession in the US provided a wider context of caution, and television was increasingly competing with cinema attendance. Hollywood studios were slow to deal effectively with the situation. The industry's insularity and patriarchal structure meant that there were few genuinely new faces, even when there were opportunities to change personnel at studios. Consequently, 'as the older generation of studio moguls aged out of the business, the only palatable exchange of power, resources, and access was one from father to son. This transition was both literal and figurative' (Montañez Smukler 2018: 44). Women like Joan Micklin Silver were far removed from such networks.

Changes in mainstream culture were also being reflected in the film industry. By 1968, the Production Code that had regulated censorship issues including nudity, language, violence and 'obscenity' was becoming increasingly difficult to implement, and was eventually abandoned. In its place, the Motion Picture Association film rating system was introduced, delivering guidance for audience suitability according to viewer age. The new system of classification opened the doors to more varied, violent and sexually explicit films. Some film studios were willing to take chances on newcomers as directors, attempting to appeal to younger audiences – and, crucially, working with smaller budgets (Lennard et al. 2022: 15–16). The so-called New Hollywood films emerged from the late 1960s, reflecting social change and the concerns of the younger generation, seeking to differentiate their culture from that of previous eras. Young American film-makers were influenced by European and other international films, which often depicted more liberal attitudes and representations of sex and nudity.

Rather than offering new opportunities for women, the industry nevertheless remained male-dominated, both behind the scenes and on screen. Film-makers who rose to prominence in this period included Francis Ford Coppola, Stanley Kubrick, Robert Altman, Arthur Penn and Martin Scorsese. Helen O'Hara pointedly wrote that: 'The New Hollywood was, immediately, extremely male, with more significant figures called Robert than women in its directorial ranks' (2021: 136). She also noted that there were few good on-screen roles for women, who were often cast as prostitutes or victims of sexual violence, whereas machismo dominated.

*Hester Street*, as we will see in the following chapters, offered a very different prospect. With a tightly buttoned, religious female protagonist and a woman as writer-director, the chances for matching mainstream appetites for exploitative sex scenes were minimal. While the subtitles, black-and-white cinematography and simple visual aesthetic of *Hester Street* resembled the European art films which were popular in the US, *Hester Street* was simply not the kind of film that was attracting American production investment in a still-precarious financial market.

Molly Haskell, in a 1975 review of *Hester Street* in the *Village Voice*, acknowledged the accomplishment of getting the film off the ground in the contemporary production environment: 'There is a huge apparatus for producing and promoting the large-scale movies and potential best sellers, and there are foundation grants for the earnest and the esoteric and the experimental, but what about the (relatively) low-budget nonforeign feature film?' (1975: 33). When Joan Micklin Silver came to seek finance for her debut feature film, she faced resistance on several fronts.

## Women making movies

In the 1960s, the number of women making movies in the US remained low compared to men, but was on the rise for the first time since the silent era. Across industries, discrimination in the workplace was being challenged in the courts. The Civil Rights Act was passed in the US in 1964, prohibiting discrimination on the basis of race, colour, religion, sex or national origin. The implementation of the Act was slow, although it marked a significant step towards workplace equality. Feminist activism in the 1970s led to some progress for women through Hollywood's professional guilds (Montañez Smukler 2018: 2). The women who started their careers as commercial film directors around the same time as Joan Micklin Silver included actor-director Lee Grant, actor-writer-director Elaine May and later, Claudia Weill. The fact that these women are Jewish reflects the vibrancy of the film-making culture within Jewish communities (discussed further below). At the time, many Jewish people worked in the entertainment industry, whereas other ethnic minorities were less represented.

Outside the mainstream movie industry, the feminist movement gave rise to ideologically and politically motivated film-making. The resulting films tended to be shown in community settings and festivals, as their production, distribution and consumption ran parallel to – but not within – the arena of commercial film-making. The first feminist film festivals in the early 1970s often screened documentaries, giving voice to women's real-life experiences, or were non-narrative and experimental in nature, tending towards an 'art' aesthetic that was countercultural and consciously in opposition to the profit-driven, Hollywood studio system (Erens 1990; Rich 1998). Micklin Silver was not actively part of the feminist film-making scene, endeavouring instead to work within the mainstream. Linda Gottlieb commented that: 'Abstract notions of feminism never interested Joan; specific women and their stories did' (Gottlieb n.d.). The separation of ideological activism from commercial industry meant that supportive networks across these different arenas were not naturally established.

While women's employment rights may have been improving, the leadership role of a film director was often not perceived to be a job for women. Micklin Silver felt it was blatant sexism when she was offered roles as a scriptwriter, but not as director (Micklin Silver 2006). Furthermore, women were excluded from the networking and mentorship opportunities which were embedded in the boys'-club culture (Montañez Smukler 2018: 44). Gottlieb recalled how she and Micklin Silver leant on each other:

We both got our stuttering starts together in the film business, and in the absence of mentors – because there were none for women in film back then – we became each other's mentors. Haltingly, fumblingly, daringly – helped mainly by Joan's husband, Raphael – we created ourselves, looking to each other for courage because there was really no one else. (Gottlieb n.d.)

It was rare for women to direct movies, but not impossible. Micklin Silver maintained belief in her abilities as a director as well as her love of film-making. Stuart Wurtzel, production designer on *Hester Street*, described the director as 'single-minded' (2024), and this quality, buoyed by Raphael's encouragement, enabled her to persist. Micklin Silver acknowledged the demands:

I'm sure lots of people quit because it is just too damn hard. It is. It's terrible. You have to lean into it all the time. I mean, you have to push at it and push at it. It's incredibly hard. But it's such a thrill to do it. I mean, to make a movie is so worth it. It's so worth every bit of it. (1979: 44)

As a woman trying to finance her first feature film, Micklin Silver was evidently at a disadvantage. But it was also the Jewish nature of *Hester Street* that deterred investors.

## A Jewish tale
Micklin Silver did not opt for a sure-fire commercial hit for her first feature as a director, but chose a story that was personally meaningful. For her, it was a question of 'if', rather than 'when', she would get the chance to direct (1979: 44). *Hester Street* was the result of a mindset that if she were to write and direct just one film, it would be one that honoured her background, especially her parents' experience of coming to America.

*Hester Street* is an explicitly Jewish story, but one which expresses universal feelings around immigration. In *The Immigrant Experience: The Long Long Journey*, Micklin Silver depicted Polish immigrants arriving in New York. She had wanted to focus on

Jewish people, but her producers rejected this as having too niche
an audience. During research, she came across Abraham Cahan's
short story *Yekl*, and decided that if she ever got the opportunity, that
would be the tale she would bring to the screen (Micklin Silver 2021
[2017]). When the film-maker sought investment for *Hester Street*,
she was again told that the story was too Jewish (McBride 1976: 7), a
judgement which raises the question of how the film's representation
of Jewish people compares to other on-screen depictions.

As has been documented widely, Jewish heritage itself has not
been a major barrier to success as a film-maker in the US (Abrams
2012; Epstein 2013; Goldman 2013). Jewish characters have been
on screen since the beginning of cinema, portrayed in both positive
and negative lights. Antisemitic stereotypes abounded in early short
British and American comedy films. When the American film-making
industry moved out from the East Coast to California in the pursuit
of better weather conditions, opportunities increased for Jewish
people, who then faced rife antisemitism that restricted entry or
advancement in several other professions. Consequently, many
early studio workers in Hollywood were Jewish, and their increased
presence in the industry led to more sympathetic portrayals on screen
(Abrams 2012: 3).

Yiddish and Jewish literature often provided source material
for films in the 1920s, with stereotypical characters emerging, such
as the stern patriarch, the rebellious son and 'the rose of the ghetto'.
In Hollywood and American-made Yiddish films during this era,
Jewish women were often portrayed positively as strong-willed and
independent, forging their own identities as American Jews (Pucker
Rivo 1998: 47). *The Jazz Singer* (dir. Alan Crosland, 1927) is perhaps
best known as one of the first movies to use synchronised sound, but
it is also significant owing to its depiction of a young Jewish man
struggling to choose between his parents' ambition for him to be
a *chazzan* (prayer leader in synagogue) and his own desire to be a
jazz performer. Its numerous remakes reflect varying contemporary
attitudes towards Jewish tradition and assimilation.

From the 1930s onwards, Jewish characters were less visible on screen. Henry Popkin analysed the erasure or disguise of Jewish characters in popular culture, describing 'the fog of concealment', which 'has fallen most heavily on the movies' (1952: 49–50). What Popkin called 'the great retreat' (ibid.: 51) of Jewish representation in the 1930s coincided with rising antisemitism in Europe. In the US, there was pressure on film-makers by Jewish organisations to exercise caution in representing Jewish characters. The Hays Code, implemented from 1934, stipulated that 'no religion shall be ridiculed', which led to a far-reaching response that, Popkin argued, effectively eliminated Jewish cultural representation. The post-war years and McCarthyism later impacted on how Jews, especially those with Russian and European roots, were depicted and perceived in mainstream culture.

The late 1960s and 1970s saw new confidence in expressing Jewish heritage, part of a wider revival of interest in exploring and celebrating cultural and ethnic roots (Diner 2000, 2011; Jacobson 2006). The American Jewish community was, on the whole, experiencing less hardship, and more professional advancement, cultural assimilation and suburban living. This put many in a stronger position to express their reflections on the past. Nathan Abrams described the reaction among artists to the silence of previous years: 'There was a determined and concerted effort to stand up for Jewish identity and to throw Jewish practices back into the face of a film culture that had ignored them or shunted them aside' (2012: 6).

Literature, stage plays, radio and films made during this period frequently dealt with questions of Jewish identity. Popular examples include novels by Philip Roth and their screen adaptations (*Goodbye, Columbus* [dir. Larry Peerce, 1969]; *Portnoy's Complaint* [dir. Ernest Lehman, 1972]); *Fiddler on the Roof* (stage musical 1964; film dir. Norman Jewison, 1971); films starring Barbra Streisand (*Funny Girl* [dir. William Wyler, 1968]; *Hello, Dolly!* [dir. Gene Kelly, 1969]; *The Way We Were* [dir. Sydney Pollack, 1973]); self-deprecating comedy by Joan Rivers, who performed regularly on *The Tonight Show* with

Johnny Carson through the 1960s and 1970s; and performances and films by Woody Allen (*Bananas*, 1971; *Sleeper*, 1973) and Mel Brooks (*The Producers*, 1967; *Blazing Saddles*, 1974). American Jewish culture in the 1970s was often characterised by comedic 'Jewish self-parody' (Erens 2008: 128) that reflected feelings of self-consciousness. A memorable example is a scene in *Annie Hall* (dir. Woody Allen, 1977) in which Alvy (Allen) eats (unkosher) ham with Annie's (Diane Keaton) Waspy family and he depicts himself as an Orthodox Hasidic Jew, wearing a fake beard. The screen splits to show Alvy's actual family, who are not Hasidic but are exaggerated, grotesque Jewish stereotypes, portrayed, as are the Hasids, in such a way as to encourage audiences to laugh *at* them, in recognition of the otherness of Jewish Americans, regardless of how they express their religion.

## Jewish women

The tone of *Hester Street* is at times light, but not comedic. Jokes and stereotypes at the expense of Jewish women were (and still are) commonplace in American culture (Antler 2007; Dundes 1985; Prell 1999). Stereotypes include the Jewish American Princess – a spoilt, uptight urbanite, seen for example in *Marjorie Morningstar* (dir. Irving Rapper, 1958) and *Goodbye, Columbus*. Another is the overbearing, overfeeding and interfering Jewish mother (and wife and mother-in-law), consolidated in popular culture by the 1964 book by Dan Greenburg, *How to be a Jewish Mother*, which sold 270,000 copies in its first year.

These pernicious stereotypes were largely propagated by Jewish men (Michel 1994; Prell 1998). Sylvia Barack Fishman interpreted their significance:

Hollywood portrayals of Jewish women (which are usually created by Jewish men) are often reflections and vicarious re-enactments of American Jewish men's rejection of their alien status, their projecting of that alien status onto Jewish women, or at the very least their unresolved relationship with their own ethnic and religious identities. (1998: 5)

American Jewish women have responded by challenging and playing with stereotypes, for example in *The Heartbreak Kid* (dir. Elaine May, 1972), *Private Benjamin* (dir. Howard Zieff, 1980), *Dirty Dancing* (dir. Emile Ardolino, 1987) and more recently by comedian Sarah Silverman, as well as in television series such as *Broad City* (2014–19) and *Crazy Ex-Girlfriend* (2015–19). These popular works instil agency and sexuality into Jewish, female characters. They do not, however, represent religiously observant women in America as *Hester Street* did. In the 1970s, depictions of Orthodoxy in America were deemed 'too Jewish' for mainstream public taste as well as for secular Jews (Bial 2005).

Micklin Silver's affection for, and pride in, Yiddish language and Jewish customs contrasted with contemporary popular images. As Patricia Erens noted, '*Hester Street* focuses on Orthodox Jewish life, a topic untreated since the late 1920s' (2008: 129). The film shone a light on aspects of Jewish heritage which many people preferred to leave in the past. The director acknowledged differing attitudes:

I've always felt there's two kinds of immigrants. One, they're a bit ashamed of it, and the experience was traumatic, and they wanna put it behind them. Well, my family wasn't like that. My family was the other kind, who enjoy talking about it, and remembering, and reveling. (Micklin Silver 2005)

## Making *Hester Street*

*Hester Street* was eventually made after Raphael Silver stepped in as producer. He had achieved success as a property developer and thought he could raise money to back his wife's project, having witnessed her disappointment at repeated rejection. Micklin Silver recalled Raphael's attitude: '[H]e got sort of angry and he saw me crawling around and he said, "You may or may not have talent but you certainly deserve the chance to find out"' (1991: 30–1).

With an initial budget of $350,000, production began in the summer of 1973 and filming took place over thirty-four days in Greenwich Village (AFI 2022). Hester Street itself was by then in a

Raphael and Joan Micklin Silver, c. late 1970s/early 1980s (courtesy Nebraska Jewish Historical Society)

predominantly Spanish-speaking area and the extensive street and shop signage would have been too costly to cover over. Nearby Morton Street was chosen as an alternative outdoor set, and dressed and filmed over four and a half days. Interior scenes were filmed at Fifth Street Stage studios, and other local buildings were used when possible (Micklin Silver and Silver 2021 [2004]). Cinematographer Kenneth Van Sickle, with whom Micklin Silver had worked previously on *The Immigrant Experience: The Long Long Journey*, was hired. The cast and crew also included many people with Jewish backgrounds. Carol Kane was cast in the lead as Gitl, after Micklin Silver had seen her perform in *Wedding in White* (dir. William Fruet, 1972), in which Kane played a teenager pregnant after rape. Stuart Wurtzel brought his experience working on stage productions, recreating the Lower East Side of 1896 on a shoestring budget. Yiddish and dialect coach Michael Gorrin was employed, because the majority of the cast did not speak any or much Yiddish.

Raphael Silver, as producer, intended to keep costs down by bringing on crew without going through the unions, who controlled hiring according to the pecking order of their lists. However, Silver agreed to raise production costs and employ through the unions, after a Teamster union leader showed him the pistol that he kept in his car (Silver 2021 [2004]). Filming finished one day ahead of schedule. Film editor Katherine Wenning and Micklin Silver worked towards a final cut, seeking advice from director Elia Kazan (*A Streetcar Named Desire*, 1951; *On the Waterfront*, 1954) and editor Ralph Rosenblum (*Goodbye, Columbus*; frequent projects with Woody Allen). By November 1974, *Hester Street* was completed (Micklin Silver and Silver 1975: 79).

Distributing the film proved to be another hurdle. Raphael Silver discovered that the common reaction among distributors was that *Hester Street* was 'A totally ethnic, Jewish film and only old Jews would see it because younger people could not relate to the story' (quoted in McBride 1976: 7). The only options proposed were to release it on the synagogue market, or in cities with large Jewish populations. Convinced that the film would be well received by diverse audiences, Silver persisted in securing wider distribution. Director John Cassavetes had experienced recent success self-distributing *A Woman Under the Influence* (1974), and this inspired Silver to reach out for advice. Cassavetes recommended Blaine Novak and Jeff Lipsky, young marketing executives with whom he had worked, to assist Silver with cinema booking and promotion.

A screening of *Hester Street* at the Dallas Film Festival in March 1975 brought positive reactions, but America-wide release did not follow immediately. *Ms.* magazine highlighted the difficulties facing independent productions at the time, including *Hester Street*: 'It's a sad story, this problem of film distribution, and it plagues not just women's films, but *all* independent ventures' (Rosen 1975: 33). The film was shown at the Cannes Film Festival in May 1975 as part of International Critics' Week, and was subsequently picked up for limited European distribution.

*Hester Street* was released in American cinemas in October 1975. A limited run in New York turned into extended runs, distribution in Los Angeles, then nationally and internationally. The film made $5 million at the box office – a resounding success considering its low budget. Carol Kane was nominated for the 1976 Academy Award for Best Actress, following a campaign headed by Max Burkett, a retired PR agent who liked to 'bet on a dark horse' (Kane quoted in Ebiri 2021). Despite losing out to Louise Fletcher (*One Flew Over the Cuckoo's Nest* [dir. Miloš Forman, 1975]), the attention brought more audiences to *Hester Street*.

Raphael and Joan formed Midwest Films to manage production and distribution themselves. The director reflected on the success of distributing *Hester Street* independently: "Course, it worked and everybody thought how smart. But at the time […] it was just […] it was desperation' (Micklin Silver 1991: 32). Creating and releasing *Hester Street* proved challenging, but the film became the foundation which cleared the path for her own work and for others after her.

Looking back in 1979 on having been told that 'woman directors are one more problem we don't need', Micklin Silver felt that the decade had already seen some progress:

Now I don't think there's a single executive that would say that to a woman director today. He might think it, but nobody would say it, so we're that step ahead. Three women have made films for studios this year. That's a lot more than any other year. Anne Bancroft and Nancy Walker and I. On the other hand, half the people in the world are women, so why wouldn't half the directors of movies be women? So, long way to go. (1979: 6)

How far have we still to go? Acknowledging women's past achievements is an important step in assessing progress, and this book intends to move us forward in that respect.

## 2 Evoking the Past in Visual and Spoken Language

*Kayn Yiddish* – No Yiddish spoken here

### Setting the scene

*Hester Street* evokes a specific place, time and culture through visual images, spoken language and music. The film's black-and-white cinematography, *mise en scène* and the treatment of language and literacy present a multilayered and multilingual cultural landscape.

As the opening credits roll, *Hester Street* begins at Joe Peltner's Dancing Academy, as a wall banner tells us. The dancers choose partners and enjoy refreshments. A subtitle specifies the setting as 'Lower East Side, New York, 1896'. The camera shows us around the lively room, the chatter and music inaudible as the soundtrack plays upbeat, non-diegetic music. Another banner states in English and Yiddish: 'No Yiddish spoken here'. Jake and Mamie (Dorrie Kavanaugh) emerge as leading characters, desirable dance partners in the crowd.

Joan Micklin Silver had a clear idea of the kind of music that would complement the film. She rejected suggestions of melancholy klezmer cello themes, instead choosing cheerful band music. The soundtrack was composed and played by William Bolcom with Gerard Schwarz, adapted from American music of the 1890s by Herbert L. Clarke. Effectively carrying optimism and hope through the film, Micklin Silver intended for the music to hold meaning: 'I want [...] music that stands for what the immigrants might have heard passing a bandstand. I mean, the America that they were longing for, the America that they wanted to become part of' (2005). The comment on 'longing' hints at an idea of something that the characters did not *yet* feel: fully part of America.

## Accents

In speech, an accent implies a trace of otherness between speaker and listener; the otherness of geographic provenance or culture. Accents can imply a speaker's linguistic difference in relation to a dominant style. Hamid Naficy developed the idea of 'accented cinema', seeking to understand shared stylistic and thematic elements between films made in different 'exilic and diasporic' circumstances around the world (2001: 3). The identification of these features requires engagement with diverse individual and group stories, while acknowledging commonalities across cultures.

Naficy proposed that accent in cinema is more likely to be connected to alternative methods of production, rather than large-budget, studio-based, mainstream film-making. In smaller-budget productions with relatively few people in positions of creative control, a film-maker may have more freedom. Joan Micklin Silver acknowledged how the production environment of *Hester Street* impacted on its tone, as there was no one limiting her creative vision, nor trying to persuade the team towards a more conventional approach, such as lessening the Yiddish content or challenging the use of black-and-white cinematography (Micklin Silver and Silver 1975: 78).

*Hester Street* grew out of Micklin Silver's identification with the Yiddish-speaking Jewish diaspora community and her interest in her family's personal histories. 'Diaspora' derives from the Greek word for scattering, and is commonly used today to describe any community dispersed from its country of origin (Clifford 1994; Cohen 1997; Safran 1991). The term, or its Hebrew equivalent *galut*, is used by Jewish communities around the world to describe their position in relation to the ancestral expulsion from the biblical land of Israel. Within these populations, there are several other later dispersed Jewish communities, such as Jews forced out of Spain, North Africa and the Middle East. Waves of nineteenth- and twentieth-century migration from Europe led to a Yiddish-speaking diaspora. Naficy distinguished between diaspora (scattering due to expulsion *or* economic/trade/family ambitions) and exile (banishment with prohibition of return), while acknowledging significant overlap between the categories and the shifting meanings over time (2001: 11–15). My focus is on ideas of accent, rather than on the overlap or distinction between diaspora and exile. *Hester Street* expresses visual, linguistic and cultural accents in multiple compositional elements.

## Black-and-white cinematography

The decision to film *Hester Street* in black and white was unusual in 1975, but not unique. Joan Micklin Silver was deeply influenced by Satyajit Ray's films, especially *Pather Panchali* (1955), the story of a poor Bengali family set in 1910, filmed in black and white. From the early days of cinema, the technology to create colour films developed, but was initially an expensive luxury. It was not until 1954 that colour films formed the majority of releases in the US (Follows 2024). Director Noah Baumbach said that black-and-white cinematography brings a form of 'instant nostalgia' (quoted in Bishop 2014). Many American films made in the 1970s used black and white as a stylistic choice to evoke the past (for example, Peter Bogdanovich's period films *The Last Picture Show*, 1971; *Paper Moon*, 1973). Woody Allen used the style in *Manhattan* (1979) to enhance the aesthetic of the film and of the city. Black-and-white cinematography can also have a distancing effect that emphasises the imaginary, surreal or thematically 'dark' content of a film, such as in *Eraserhead* (dir. David Lynch, 1977).

Micklin Silver and the production team consulted library archives and exhibitions to study photographs depicting life in the Lower East Side in the 1890s, especially the social documentary photographs by Jacob Riis and Lewis Hine (Micklin Silver 1979: 15; 2005). These images had been reproduced across America through the 1960s and were familiar to many Americans (Diner 2000: 79–85). The director believed that black-and-white cinematography would effectively evoke Jake and Gitl's world and capture the gloom of the tenement interiors: there were more than 200,000 rooms without natural light and ventilation in Manhattan in 1903, with most of them concentrated in the Jewish district (Matłoka 2015: 84).

Daytime foot traffic on Hester Street, *c.* 1890. Photograph by Jacob Riis (Getty Images)

Hester Street, 1898. Photograph by Byron Company, New York (Museum of the City of New York/Getty Images); Lower East Side tailor shop, c. 1900. Photograph by Jacob Riis (Bettmann/Getty Images)

Market day in the Jewish quarter of East Side, New York City, 1912.
Photograph by Lewis Hine (The Miriam and Ira D. Wallach Division of Art,
Prints and Photographs: Photograph Collection, The New York Public Library)

The cinematography is also reminiscent of the popular Yiddish films made between the 1910s and 1930s. Yiddish-language cinema was an effective way for speakers to maintain transatlantic, diasporic culture, with exchanges of films between cities including New York, Minsk and Warsaw (Hoberman 1995). *Hester Street* bears traces of multiple pasts and places: 1896, pre-war Yiddish cinema and the time of its making. One effect is to heighten the feeling that *Hester Street* carries a rich cultural history to audiences, bringing stories from one generation to another.

### Life in a tenement apartment
Overcrowding and poverty were prevalent in the Lower East Side in 1896, when Cahan wrote *Yekl*.[1] The *mise en scène* of *Hester Street* shows domestic life in the tenements. Jake and Gitl's small home is furnished modestly with useful objects, and several scenes are set in the parlour/kitchen, where Jake used to sleep and now occupied

by Mr Bernstein (Mel Howard). The set design supports Naficy's observation that accented cinema can feature 'claustrophobic interiors, often ethnically coded' (2001: 289). The table is surrounded by a clutter of kitchenware, a sewing machine, candlesticks for Sabbath and festivals, hanging clothes and books belonging to Mr Bernstein. The candlesticks are 'ethnically coded' symbols of Jewish observance, often the most precious items in a Jewish home. The books are, in Naficy's terms, 'Motivated props: Fetishized objects and icons of homeland and of past' (ibid.). For Mr Bernstein and Gitl, the religious texts represent the desirable study of the Torah (the Hebrew Bible comprising the Five Books of Moses) and a connection to a religious life that is more difficult to pursue in New York. Books are hinted to be fetished objects by Mr Bernstein, who explains that he could not remain a scholar in Russia because he struggled to concentrate on Torah study, thinking instead about 'profanities' (women).

The characters are surrounded by writing. Shelves are decorated with bunting, made out of Yiddish-language newspapers; in the market, Jake buys Yossele some snacks from a street vendor which are wrapped in newspaper. Production designer Stuart Wurtzel explained that residents of the tenements would make decorations out of anything to hand, and the only items cheaply available and abundant in New York at the time were newspapers (2024).

## Language and literacy

Yiddish and English are the principal spoken languages in *Hester Street*. As well as translation subtitles, images of texts and references to Aramaic and Hebrew evoke the multiplicity of languages that characterised the Lower East Side, and emphasise the problems of communication that new immigrants faced. The written word features prominently, increasing the spectator's visual engagement with the screen.

Reading and illiteracy are significant themes in *Hester Street*. When Jake receives a letter from home, he takes it to a *sofer* (scribe) to be read for him. The letter contains news of his father's death, but the scribe will not read the exact text aloud, as it is against Jewish tradition to announce the news of death in this way. Instead, he says, 'Blessed is the true Judge', which Jake understands to mean that a family member has died. Letters and 'native script' are often featured in accented films (Naficy 2001: 5, 289). Jake's letter is framed in close-up so that we can see the handwriting, emphasising the written word. In 1896 it was common, for women especially, to be illiterate (Stahl Weinberg 1988). Gitl's illiteracy is evident from her admiration of Mr Bernstein and her delight when he teaches Yossele (Paul Freedman) the Hebrew alphabet. The moments depicting illiteracy in *Hester Street* are reminders of the rapid social progress over the twentieth century.

The issue of illiteracy is acknowledged by Jewish religious authorities. Certain texts and documents must (to this day) be read aloud, as occurs towards the end of the film at the reading of the *get* (divorce agreement). Both the *ketubah* (marriage certificate) and the *get* are written in Hebrew script in Aramaic, the technical legal language of Jewish Talmudic law, dominant from the time of the Babylonian Exile in the 6th century BCE until the early medieval period. The American immigration official who questions Jake

and Gitl does not know which way up to hold their *ketubah* – in a moment that shows mutual incomprehension.

The linguistic multiplicity in *Hester Street* reflects the absorption of different languages into Jewish life and liturgy. Classical Hebrew is used in the Torah, in prayer and presumably in some of Mr Bernstein's books. Additionally, various Hebrew scripts can be seen in *Hester Street*, as some handwritten texts, such as Jake's letter, use 'script' (akin to cursive in English), while 'block' (similar to capital letters) can be seen in print and on street signs. Within Bernstein's books, we can presume that there is also 'Rashi script', a typeface based on a Sephardic semi-cursive script, used in print since the late fifteenth century. Mr Bernstein's literacy and knowledge of English demonstrate his cultural fluency.

Naficy emphasised the importance of language in accented films. If faced with loss or deterioration of their original language in new countries, 'many accented filmmakers doggedly insist on writing the dialogues in their original language – to the detriment of the film's wider distribution. However, most accented films are bilingual, even multilingual, multivocal, and multiaccented' (2001: 24). As noted in the previous chapter, the Yiddish content of *Hester Street* did put off some potential distributors. Yet the popular appetite for the film was likely, in part, due to the unusual linguistic content, as viewers of many backgrounds could relate to the optimistic intent to revoice accents of the past.

## Yiddish

In 1896, when *Hester Street* is set, varieties of Yiddish were spoken by Ashkenazi Jewish people across Europe, including in the Pale of Settlement in the western Russian Empire, where Jews were permitted to settle from 1791 to 1917. Yiddish (which means 'Jewish') is widely thought to have originated in French and Northern Italian Jewish communities as they moved north and settled in German-speaking areas of the Rhine Basin in the early Middle Ages, and spread further as the Crusades forced many people out of the region

(YIVO 2014: 3). Yiddish absorbed some Slavic linguistic elements and was influenced by the Hebrew and Aramaic used in Jewish ritual. Evidently, 'Yiddish is a non-territorial language' (Pasikowska-Schnass 2022: 2). Some Jewish people would also – or only – be fluent in their national language. Not all Jewish immigrants to America in the 1890s were Orthodox, and speaking Yiddish was not an indicator of religious practice.

Between 1880 and 1900, the population of New York grew by over two million (Gregory 2022), as immigrants fled persecution and pogroms or came in search of better living conditions, work opportunities and often to join family members. The US was already home to long-established Jewish communities, many with origins in Germany, and Sephardic Jews with Spanish and Portuguese backgrounds who had arrived after the Inquisition, often via South America. At the turn of the twentieth century, an estimated 250,000 Jews lived in the Lower East Side of New York (Antler 1995: 181).

Like Micklin Silver's parents, Jake and Gitl come from Russia. Mamie is from Poland and immigrated when she was sixteen, now speaking English 'like a regular Yankee'. Author Abraham Cahan was born in Lithuania in 1860, settling in New York after arriving in Philadelphia in 1882. The film does not show life in *der heim* (the homeland), whereas in Cahan's *Yekl*, there is a reminiscent description of village life, and a reference to the Russian government's 'redoubled discrimination against the sons of Israel' (Cahan 1896: 9–10). In the Russian Empire, rulings made between 1881 and 1905 restricted Jewish people's trade, residency, property ownership and entry into professions. Tens of thousands of Jews were expelled from several cities (Polonsky 2010; Stahl Weinberg 1988). Jake represents those immigrants who saw America as a beacon of new beginnings. Such an attitude was encapsulated by Vilnius-born Jewish poet Judah Leib Gordon, whose 1882 poem 'My Sister Ruhama' (written in Hebrew) called on Russian Jewry to emigrate, principally to the United States: 'Arise, let us go! Where the light of freedom / Shines on all men and brightens all souls, / Where all creatures of God are loved the same, / No insults are waged 'gainst one's nation or one's faith' (translated and quoted in Stanislawski 1988: 199).

New York's Lower East Side became the epicentre of a thriving Yiddish-speaking community that generated literature, theatre and later, cinema. As well as writing fiction, Cahan co-founded the Yiddish-language socialist newspaper *Forvertz* (*Forward*) in 1897, becoming its editor-in-chief until 1946. The effect of such a prolific culture was that the Yiddish language influenced the American vernacular (Steinmetz 2001). But some people, like Jake, felt that Yiddish bore traces of a life of oppression and eschewed its use in the New World. The Holocaust later devastated European Yiddish life, as a majority of the six million Jewish people who perished would have been Yiddish speakers. This loss reverberated in diaspora communities who felt the obliteration of their places and cultures of origin (Diner 2000). The use of Yiddish in *Hester Street* evokes complex attitudes towards a language that many people associate with both vitality and destruction.

Joan Micklin Silver herself did not speak Yiddish fluently, although she was surrounded by the language:

You know, my mother's family, and my father used to sit around and talk in Yiddish and tell stories of the old country, and who came, and who left, and who went crazy, and who went back, and who, you know, all these wonderful stories. And a lot of times they would tell them in English, but they'd get to the punch line, and that would be in Yiddish, and my mother would try to translate, and then she would say, 'Well, it really doesn't translate.' (2005)

In 1943, Isaac Bashevis Singer similarly described the untranslatability of Yiddish:

A great number of Yiddish words and phrases are so tightly bound to the old country that, when used here, they appear not only to be imported from another land, but borrowed from a completely alien conceptual system, half obliterated by time. (1989 [1943]: 8)

Singer was born in 1903 near Warsaw and fled to New York in 1935. He continued to write short stories and novels in Yiddish, believing in the language's strengths but also aware of its limitations in America. In 1978, Singer won the Nobel Prize for Literature. Micklin Silver recognised Singer's influence in *Crossing Delancey*, through book-loving protagonist Isabelle who enthusiastically praises the writer. Singer described how, by 1943, Yiddish seemed to be a receptacle of the past:

Our mother tongue has grown old. The mother is already a grandmother and a great grandmother. She wandered with us from Germany to Poland, Russia, Rumania. Now she is in America, but in spirit she still lives in the old country – in her memories. [...] When she starts talking about the past (through the mouth of a true talent), pearls drop from her lips. She remembers what happened fifty years ago better and more clearly than what happened this morning. (Ibid.: 12)

It is significant that Singer emphasises the femininity of the 'mother tongue', as in *Hester Street*, Gitl is the principal speaker of Yiddish – it is her arrival that leads to its dominance in the film, until she is more fluent in English. Speaking English proficiently was considered a sign of success (as Jake would say, no longer being a 'greenhorn'), but *Hester Street* suggests that sometimes only Yiddish will do.

## Yiddish-American

*Hester Street* is imbued with a Yiddish-American accent that evokes the past not only through speech but also through imagery. The film's precise location in Hester Street asserts its status as American, constructing a confident presentation of Yiddish-Jewish-American hybridity. *Hester Street* combines cinematic traditions with Yiddish and Jewish visual and linguistic elements, creating an accented style that reflects Micklin Silver's multiple influences.

The film's accented style and voice are also shaped by Micklin Silver's position as a woman in the film industry. *Hester Street* shows aspects of women's lives that have been overlooked in dominant, patriarchal cultural history. Sydney Stahl Weinberg in *The World of Our Mothers* elucidated the climate of historical study that prevailed until the 1980s:

It is difficult to retrieve a sense of the lives of ordinary women in cultures that have changed or disappeared. In most societies, the vast majority of women like my grandmother were too busy with day-to-day tasks to leave such records as memoirs or diaries, even if they had all been literate. Most were not joiners or activists and seldom entered the written record or history books. Statistics can tell us where women settled or what jobs they held, but little about how they viewed their own lives. Thus, until recently, the history of immigration has been the story of men, with the role of women emerging, if at all, only peripherally. (1988: xiii)

*Hester Street* gives voice to Jewish immigrant women's experiences in their own languages: Yiddish and accented English. Naficy pointed out the importance of historicisation in accented films which attempt 'to recount and account for personal/national past' (2001: 290). *Hester Street* deals with intergenerational, personal, ethnic, religious and national past. Forming part of a 1970s cultural revival that witnessed interest in women's stories, including the reprinting of literature by Polish-born Jewish American writer Anzia Yezierska, the film leads us to ask what role cinema can play in keeping language and culture alive. The next chapter takes us deeper into the Lower East Side.

## 3 Place and Movement: Immigration and Point of View

In Hester-st. [...] drygoods and the like are sold during the earlier part of the week, while Thursday afternoon and night and Friday until the Sabbath sets in the odor of fish, the clamor of the venders and the shrill bargaining of the housewives fill the air. At night this scene is lighted by great torches attached to the carts. It is not an American city any longer. The idea of it being New-York is unbelievable to an uptown visitor who sees it for the first time.

(*New-York Tribune* 1901: 8)

Hester Street was the heart of the Lower East Side, a bustling market street inhabited and frequented by Yiddish-speaking Jews. The street was nicknamed ironically 'Chazer Mark' (pig market) in Yiddish, for there you could buy anything but pigs, which Jews are forbidden to eat (Blumenson 1950: 65). Hester Street itself is not named in Cahan's *Yekl*, which describes nearby Suffolk Street in detail. By 1975, many Jewish residents had moved out of the area and into the surrounding suburbs, but Hester Street had become famous, a synecdoche for the Lower East Side and a Jewish way of life during a particular era. The specific location is emphasised by the film's title, chosen rather than *Yekl* or *Gitl* (which would have responded to Cahan's protagonist-title model).

The Lower East Side became 'American Jewry's central sacred space' (Diner 2000: 37) over the second half of the twentieth century. The area was a focal point even for those whose relatives had not resided there, as the generation of the immigrants' children – including Joan Micklin Silver – sought to connect to their heritage and to evoke a collective past. The film-maker's parents both came from Russia as children, her mother's family settling in Kansas City, Missouri, and her father's in Omaha, Nebraska (Micklin Silver 2005).

*Hester Street* encapsulates the experiences of many immigrants regardless of the specifics of their journeys, with the effect that the film contributed to the Lower East Side becoming 'the cultural metaphor for any place in America where Jewish traditionalism inevitably clashed with American opportunities' (Diner 2000: 31).

*Hester Street* is set entirely in New York and features well-known places, including the street market, Ellis Island and Central Park, as well as interior scenes of Jake and Gitl's tenement apartment. Tensions around social, religious and national identity are played out within the narrow geographic circles in which the characters reside and work. The theme of movement underpins the film. The protagonists share a common background, having moved from their homelands to America, with the hope of it being their *goldene medina* (golden land). The relocation informs their internal, psychological movement as they acclimatise to new identities.

The immigrants have lived in America for differing lengths of time, and each demonstrates a different perspective towards their surroundings (as discussed in Chapter 5). *Hester Street*, like *Yekl*, begins according to Jake's point of view. After Gitl's arrival, the emphasis shifts to favour Gitl's perspective. *Hester Street* presents locations in relation to the protagonists, expressing perspectives through interactions with place. By analysing key scenes at specific locations, we can see how physical, psychological and cinematic movement are linked.

## Hester Street

We are first shown Hester Street outdoor market early in the film, as Jake steps out of his workshop, into the market and walks home. Jake walks to the right, and a horse and cart travel from right to left: Hester Street is a thoroughfare. The camera tilts slightly upwards, just enough for us to see a shop sign advertising marble baths, written in English and Yiddish. Jake's eyes fall upon a window displaying a poster with details of steamship tickets for Bremen (a principal German port) to New York. Jake seems to briefly consider this poster, although we have not yet been made aware that he would be thinking of his wife and son who await their tickets for passage. Jake catches sight of a reflection of two young women and turns, the camera following his line of sight to show them returning his gaze. Tweaking his moustache, Jake smiles as the women recede into Hester Street, then walks jauntily towards home. The camera tracks along the street as Jake passes sellers who display fabrics, hats and other wares. He buys a new hat and soon arrives at his door, where he is met by Mrs Kavarsky (Doris Roberts), who brings news of his landlady's illness and the letter from Russia. For Jake, Hester Street offers exciting opportunity and is a place where travel, socialising and leisure are available. This first Hester Street scene is bookended by sequences that reveal the constraints Jake experiences indoors, at work and in his rented room.

The second street scene occurs once Gitl and Yossele have joined Jake in New York. Before Yossele leaves the apartment with his father, Gitl puts salt in his pockets to ward off evil, a ritual that emphasises a boundary between inside and outside. The excursion shows Hester Street according to Yossele.

The market is now introduced with a shot tilting slightly downwards, showing the width and depth of the street and people's movement in all directions. The camera focuses on other children and objects that would have caught a child's eye. We see children as they play on travelling and stationary carts, among the stalls and eating. Hester Street, from this perspective, is a playground. Rapid cuts in the editing convey the business of the street where fruit, chickens, fabrics and clothes are sold, and many of the traders chat to Jake and Yossele. Hester Street is a friendly place. As horse-drawn carts pass by, Jake takes the opportunity to teach his son, translating the everyday sights from Yiddish to English. The sounds of the market are audible but the soundtrack is here dominated by cheerful non-diegetic music, which ends abruptly when Joe Peltner stops Jake and enquires about his son – whom Jake has not previously mentioned.

The back and forth of the horses was creatively staged, as the budget allowed for only one horse – who was the most expensive performer of all, with strict limitations on working hours and requiring a handler. The horse was painted entirely, and as the colour gradually wore off, was filmed patchy and then plain as it walked in different directions, with the result that it looked like several different horses at work (Micklin Silver and Silver 2021 [2004]).

The third street scene is short. Jake and Mr Bernstein walk home with their sewing machines over their shoulders as they suddenly find themselves unemployed. Mrs Kavarsky is waiting at the entrance to their tenement building so that she can keep Mr Bernstein and Yossele outside while Gitl unveils her new look to Jake. With this scene, we are reminded of the geographic blend of social and personal problems: unemployment, sexual desire, marital concerns and other matters are visible from the street and played out on the communal doorstep.

The fourth and final scene of Hester Street is a backdrop to Gitl's broadening horizons following her divorce from Jake, at the film's conclusion (discussed further in Chapter 5). In this scene, Jake and Mamie walk off to City Hall to get married. They are filmed from above, with the camera situated in an upper-floor window (as this was cheaper than hiring a crane, although more cramped) (Micklin Silver and Silver 1975: 79). Once the couple has exited,

Gitl and Mr Bernstein round the corner and enter Hester Street, with Yossele walking between the two. The trio walk down the centre of the street and the camera pulls back to get a wider view. Gitl and Mr Bernstein are discussing how to invest their money and what kind of business they will run in the future. They continue to walk along Hester Street, towards the camera, and remain centre frame. The camerawork suggests that Hester Street is 'theirs', emphasising Gitl's sense of belonging by the end of the film. They exit to the lower right of the frame, which freezes as the film cuts to the end credits. Gitl, Mr Bernstein and Yossele are fixed within Hester Street, part of its fabric, their futures tied up within the small area of opportunity.

## Ellis Island

The immigration centre at Ellis Island is another location which is part of American cultural memory, and Gitl and Yossele's arrival there marks a turning point in the film. Ellis Island started operating in 1892, and between then and its closure in 1952, more than twelve million immigrants passed through its gates at a rate of up to 5,000 a day. It was a place of tension, anticipation, disappointment and confusion, dubbed the 'Island of Tears' as it was where immigrants who were permitted entry were separated from loved ones who failed inspection, and were sent back to their country of origin (Polland and Soyer 2012: 5). Unable to afford the costs of filming at the site of Ellis Island, the production team instead used Tweed Courthouse in Chambers Street, Manhattan (Micklin Silver and Silver 2021 [2004]). The depiction of the immigration process echoes parallel scenes in Micklin Silver's *The Immigrant Experience: The Long Long Journey*.

We see Jake climb the stairs of a grand building, confused as he looks around. Jake approaches double doors with small windows, through which he can see and hear people in the holding room. He moves slowly in the dark, in contrast to the movement, noise and light on the other side. The doors open and the camera follows Jake into the hall. A large American flag hangs overhead, and a wire fence keeps the 'unprocessed' immigrants to one side. In this sequence, we

frequently see Jake from the back and side of his head rather than straight on, heightening anticipation. Is he perhaps remembering his own arrival in America? The camera pans to follow Jake as he looks for his family, then cuts back and forth from him to Yossele, who waits on a bench, tension building as father and son do not recognise each other after three years' separation. Gitl is framed in close-up as she sits, looking rather helpless, next to Yossele, her wide eyes scanning the hectic room. A subsequent frame shows Gitl in medium close-up, her identity paper label around her neck and bundle of belongings close by.

The images of Gitl, Jake and Yossele are interspersed with other families talking across the dividing barriers, touching fingers through the bars in acts of intimacy which will be contrasted by Jake's frosty reception towards his family. The camera position alternates between Jake's and Gitl's side of the barrier. Gitl stands up and calls out, 'Yankl!' (Jake's equivalent Yiddish name, diminutive of Yekl). She looks very happy, but Jake, on the other side, looks confused. As they come face to face, Gitl realises that her husband has shaved off his beard. The family walk on either side of the divide to reunite physically, but Gitl and Yossele are pushed back by an official in uniform.

The family is then questioned, before admittance is granted. The processing room is marked with multiple barriers and the immigration officers are situated at a higher level than the new immigrants. This is reflected in the framing of Jake, Gitl and Yossele, who are shot from above to imply that they are being looked down upon by the authorities. The camera angle seems to diminish Gitl, who is positioned in the background, small like her young son, who is held at her face height: they do not understand what is being said and are powerless in this situation. Gitl's eyes respond when the immigration official laughs at Jake and Gitl, as although she does not comprehend the words, she ascertains his tone.

Gitl is asked to produce their *ketubah* and passes Yossele to Jake while she searches for the document. In a moment of anger at this point of urgency and frustration, Jake strikes the child. In Cahan's *Yekl*, it is Yossele who loses his temper while Jake tries to kiss his son. This shift in *Hester Street* encourages audience sympathy to move away from Jake. Carol Kane's face is framed and lit to emphasise her expressive eyes and signals the transfer of point of view that takes place at Ellis Island. The change of perspective is symbolically linked to the location of the immigration centre, which is itself a place of transfer and of shift in identity for the people who successfully passed through it.

Naficy observed that accented cinema often depicts '[t]ransnational border spaces', such as 'airports and seaports, train and bus stations' (2001: 238–9). Ellis Island is one such border space. The scenes here in *Hester Street* foreground physical borders, such as doors, windows and wire divisions. While not shown on screen, the borders of the sea – the American coast and around the island – are implicit. Language presents another barrier encountered by Gitl on her arrival.

Although Jake and Gitl live together after being reunited in New York, the ways in which they interact with space and location are significantly different.

## Jake's spaces

Jake is mercurial and often in movement. He is physically imposing and seems to dominate his space with his confident gesticulation and noise, often laughing or shouting. Like many Jewish residents of the Lower East Side, Jake works in a cramped sweatshop at a sewing machine, but he revels in freedom of movement in social spaces. Jake's exuberant sensuality is communicated through his locations of leisure. He is first shown in the dance school (filmed in a local Ukrainian hall). Jake pursues a physically intimate relationship with Mamie, stealing kisses in stairwells and rooftops, as they have no private place of their own. Before Gitl arrives in New York, Jake and Mamie go up to her apartment building's roof to enjoy time alone together, only to find several other people lying among the billowing laundry, escaping the hot, cramped apartments. Jake's pursuit of pleasure leads him to his regular prostitute (in one of many scenes not found in Cahan's book). Jake delights at being outdoors in Central Park, where he teaches his son to play baseball.

## Gitl's spaces

Gitl appears to occupy a smaller world than Jake, as she is mostly shown in the home. Their bedroom becomes an important setting

for exploring her identity in a new country and where she will experiment with clothing and hairstyles. It is interesting that her arrival is preceded not only by the death of Jake's father in Russia (whom she would have looked after), but also the hospitalisation – and implied subsequent death – of the landlady. Gitl therefore is installed into a new housekeeping role, picking up the reins from the landlady. She is repeatedly praised for cooking and cleaning, her home becoming a source of pride.

We see Gitl expand her knowledge from within the kitchen. As she prepares food, Gitl asks her son to teach her English, repeating aloud 'stove' and 'lunch'. When the men come home, Jake makes Mr Bernstein and Gitl say 'good evening' to each other in English. The kitchen table is important as the centre of gathering and exchange. Here, she hears Jake and Mr Bernstein discussing whether Yossele could grow up to be president – discovering that the lodger knows the president must be American-born, according to the Constitution. The table is also the setting for Mr Bernstein to teach Yossele to read Hebrew, as well as where Gitl and Mr Bernstein eventually declare their commitment to one another, across piles of books. Gitl travels internally, despite the limited space.

## Central Park

A pivotal scene that reflects the worldviews of Jake, Gitl and Mr Bernstein is their trip to Central Park. They enter with Yossele, running and laughing through dappled sunlight between the trees, and the soundtrack plays jaunty piano music. The sense of space that contrasts with their usual life in the tenement buildings is emphasised by the camera pan down a huge tree, under which they sit with a picnic, Mr Bernstein with some books. At this point in the film, Gitl's English has improved enough for her to converse relatively fluently. As Jake stands and eats, he exclaims triumphantly:

| | |
|---|---|
| JAKE | Look what a place is America, *nu* Bernstein. |
| […] | |
| BERNSTEIN | Here one must take a train for an hour just to be near a tree. |
| JAKE | So go back to Russia. Here, a Jew is a *mensch*. In Russia we was afraid to walk within ten feet of a gentile. |
| GITL | Yankl, where in America is the gentiles, uh? I go with Mrs Kavarsky Rivington St, Delancey St, everywhere Jews. The gentiles keep in another place, huh. […] |

JAKE        You know what the trouble is with you, Gitl? Look on me, give a look on me: Am I a Jew or a gentile? Forget that you know me, just by what you see, what do you say?

BERNSTEIN        A Jew is a Jew.

JAKE        What do you know?

GITL        Mr Bernstein knows many things. He going to give lessons in how to talk English.

BERNSTEIN        I'm looking for new students all the time, 25 cents an hour.

JAKE        I'll be goddam. Who'd want to take lessons from such a greeny? Look at him. Bernstein, you want my advice? Go to the *shadchan* [matchmaker], say I'll take what you've got – deaf, hunchback, as long as she got money. Then, you buy yourself a little store, let the hunchback run the place, and you can sit in the back all day and read the books, huh, what do you say?

The setting and conversation reveal the diverse perspectives within the group, which are representative of prevalent attitudes within many Jewish communities (Pally 1984). It is significant that the discussion occurs outdoors, which seems to enable reflection on their status in America. Jake expresses happily that he doesn't think he looks like a Jew. His self-consciousness is revealed through his acknowledgement that: 'In Russia we was afraid to walk within ten feet of a gentile': in America, he is valued as a *mensch* (a good man) and is no longer afraid. Rubinow, writing in 1902–3 about the Russian Jewish community in New York, provides evidence that Jake's was a common mindset: 'we observe among New York Jews a cheerfulness and a manifestation of joy and elation which is so unusual among the Jews in Russia' (1959 [1902–3]: 99).

Mr Bernstein recognises that manner of dress makes no difference to someone's Jewishness. To him, it does not matter where one lives or how one is perceived externally, as he unapologetically feels Jewish wherever he is. Gitl, making a wise observation, is confused about the geographic and social position of Jews in America. She implies that despite Jake's posturing, he moves only within very limited circles. *Hester Street* does not depict antisemitic attitudes encountered in wider America, only the insularity and size of the Jewish community in the Lower East Side.

Central Park is emblematic as a public, communal space, often featured in literary and cinematic depictions of New York. In *Hester Street*, the 'central' space seems disconnected geographically from the daily life of the protagonists, as we haven't seen how they got there, no familiar landmarks are shown and there is no one else in view. These elements emphasise the sense that the protagonists live in a bubble and lack integration into wider society. Nonetheless, they are now American, and identify as such, speaking English and discussing their perceptions of being Jewish Americans.

## Transitional zones

Due to budget constraints when making *Hester Street*, the filming locations, sets and props were limited. There are no expensive scenes depicting Russia or international journeys. The focus is on the protagonists' internal, psychological movement as they go about their present, daily lives. The minimal geographic movement reflects the new immigrants' limited horizons.

After having crossed the national border at Ellis Island, the characters in *Hester Street* live in an area that was a hybrid cultural border. Hasia Diner described the function of the Lower East Side for the immigrant residents, evoking the biblical narrative of freedom:

In a kind of transitional zone, they underwent an ordeal of cultural reeducation as they learned to be free. The Lower East Side served as that metaphoric middle ground where Jews dwelled among themselves while waiting for permission to enter the real America. It served as their narrow bridge between slavery and freedom, between the Egypt of Russia and Poland and the promised land of America. (2000: 20)

The ideas of promise and freedom chime with Micklin Silver's aim for the music to convey longing. Naficy observed that border aesthetics often include multifocality and multiple subjectivity (2001: 290), elements which are prominent in *Hester Street*. Multifocality occurs in the depictions of the market street according to the subjective point of view of Jake, Yossele and Gitl. The main transition in cinematic subjectivity, from Jake to Gitl, occurs significantly at the border point of Ellis Island, the gateway to America for millions of immigrants.

Hester Street was geographically in New York but culturally foreign – at least at the first glance of an outsider, as the 1901 *New-York Tribune* article opined. With *Hester Street*, Micklin Silver demonstrates that the market may have seemed foreign, but for its residents, what was going on internally, psychologically, was Americanisation – each immigrant adjusting to their geographic movement with corresponding psychological movement, at differing paces and in different ways. In life, such movement is not always visible to an observer, but film enables us to glimpse into internal worlds, especially through close-ups and interior, domestic scenes.

Movement can also be understood in terms of temporal shifts. *Hester Street* strengthens the mythology of a place which was once – but no longer by the 1970s – the epicentre of a 'Promised Land' for immigrant Jews (Cahan 1896: 12; Rubinow 1959 [1902–3]: 92). Other new immigrant communities were then living on Hester Street, as noted in the *New York Times* in 1975: 'Few Jews live on Hester today. Some Italian-Americans remain and there are still many Puerto Ricans. But Hester Street's tomorrow, which has already begun today, is clearly Chinese-American' (Shepard 1975: 66). These observations emphasise the movement of different immigrant groups in and out of the area. By centring on one well-known street that housed various communities over time, Micklin Silver appeals to diverse cinema audiences who may connect with the wider immigrant experience and not only to the particular struggles of Jewish people.

The neighbourhood was a location of psychological journeys, where immigrants navigated how much of the old world they brought into the new. The next chapter takes a closer look at Jewish rituals and customs, asking how and why they are represented in *Hester Street*.

# **4** Uncovering: The Symbolism of Costume and Ritual

'It hurts? That means it's working.'

Mrs Kavarsky

The characters of *Hester Street* are faced with Americanisation, negotiating which traditions to maintain or let go as they arrive in New York. While European, Orthodox, Jewish costume and ritual may be culturally specific, the process of adjustment is common to many immigrants, providing an accessible point of connection.

To understand the attitudes and lifestyle depicted in the film, it is worth noting that adaptation of Jewish practice is not prohibited per se, but for Orthodox Jews must be approved by their Rabbinic authorities. Jewish practice is governed by rules and rituals relating to all aspects of life. Obligatory rules are dictated by *Halacha* (law), derived from the Torah and codified in the Talmud (compiled between 200 and 800 CE) as *dat Moshe* (from the law of Moses). Many traditions derive from later eras, adapted according to geography, community and in relation to the contemporary mores of non-Jewish host cultures. Customs are known as *minhag*, including *minhag hamakom* (according to the custom of place) and *dat Yehudit* (according to the custom of Jewish women). The ways in which rules, rituals and traditions are practised have changed over time and place, to some extent, and various sections of the Jewish community uphold them in different ways, observing some rules more strictly than others. The Americanisation of the characters in *Hester Street* should therefore not be interpreted to mean that they are necessarily breaking or acting against Jewish law. Rather, their negotiation of how to be Jewish in America marks one stage in a long history of diasporic religious adaptation.

*Hester Street* does not depict the routine rituals of Sabbath and festival observance which are often shown on screen, such as lighting candles or attending synagogue. Rather, we see Gitl and Jake grapple with deciding if and how they want to represent their Jewishness day to day through covering or uncovering their bodies and hair. The issue of Gitl's head-covering symbolises all the differences between Gitl and Jake. Indeed, the narrative tension builds around her head-covering, reaching a crescendo when her natural hair is revealed.

Jewish studies scholar Shaina Hammerman devoted considerable attention to the significance of Gitl's head-covering in her reading of *Hester Street*. However, her analysis is undermined by errors, such as knowingly conflating general Haredi (strictly Orthodox) with the specific group of Hasidic people (a branch of Orthodoxy concerned with mysticism and spirituality), and describing Gitl's *sheitl* (wig) as realistic, looking 'so much like the real thing it is there to conceal' (2018: 117). However, Hammerman does raise some useful points, suggesting that 'Hasidic performances materialize as crucial components for understanding unspoken anxieties about the Jewish position on the national landscape' (ibid.: xxv). This chapter presents an opportunity for a more nuanced understanding of Jewish custom and the 'unspoken anxieties' that the characters of *Hester Street* embody. Analysis of religious and cinematic performance, particularly in relation to expectations for men and women, can help us to recognise Micklin Silver's voice as a Jewish, female film-maker.

## Men's clothing and hair

The symbolic weight of head covering for Jewish men is expressed early in *Hester Street*, well before Gitl arrives, when the friends chat over drinks at the end of an evening. Jake and Mamie flirt and discuss their boarding arrangements. Mamie reveals that she has saved up some money and now sleeps in the parlour with her landlady's two daughters. Jake boasts that he has his own bed – soon admitting that it is a lounge chair rather than a bed. Jake is impressed by Mamie's independent outlook and ambition, or maybe simply by her savings. The conversation tells us that the characters may be ambitious and upwardly mobile, but they live in cramped conditions with little luxury. At this point, a new character enters: Shloimy Navarsky (Zane Lasky), who has just arrived in New York. The friends simultaneously welcome and deride Shloimy, commenting on his bad smell. Despite his teasing, Jake is friendly and orders some tea for the new arrival. Jake then takes Shloimy's hat and puts it on his own head, while the friends laugh and clap at the new-old-look Jake – for he, too, would have once worn a similar hat.

Still wearing Shloimy's hat, Jake addresses him in Yiddish: '*Nu*, how do you like America?' Shloimy replies that he is looking for his cousin, but Jake says to his friends (not addressing Shloimy directly) that he will soon learn there is no such thing as relatives in America. When his tea arrives, Shloimy wants his hat back so that he can say a *bracha* (blessing) before drinking. Once his head is re-covered and the tea is blessed, the friends pronounce *mazal tov* (congratulations). This scene reveals Jake's complex relationship with religious head covering: he derides Shloimy, yet also takes the hat for himself, seemingly as a joke but in the knowledge that this would upset the religious newcomer.

Jake's friends laugh when he puts on the hat as it is reminiscent of the old, un-American, greenhorn ways. Significantly, the friends' conversation has just told us that they too are finding their feet as immigrants to New York. Shloimy's hat is a wearable, portable item from the old world. It is a transferable symbol of traditional Jewishness, to the extent that when Jake takes it, we hear him speak Yiddish for the first time. Jake becomes or, rather, performs a version of his former self. The effect of Jake wearing the hat is that we see it as a costume that can easily be put on and taken off: one which Shloimy needs, but Jake wants to play with. The scene puts into relief that Jake and possibly his friends (who may also have had Orthodox upbringings) have made the positive choice to leave religious observance, to shed their old ways as they left their old country. Jake has ditched the religious head-covering, the language and the ritual.

Although Shloimy is a figure of fun for the American friends, he is also immediately welcomed. The similarities and differences are emphasised especially through statements on what it means to be American. There may be 'no such thing as relatives', but as Mamie points out, Shloimy can have two sugars in his tea – 'Why not? This is America.' The comments suggest an anxiety about how American they really feel. Bringing this anxiety to the fore, Shloimy is an embodiment of their past, reminding the friends of their own immigration. Shloimy, who does not appear again, is a doppelgänger who traditionally symbolises the return of the repressed and imminent loss (Freud 1955 [1919]; Vardoulakis 2006). His arrival foreshadows Gitl's, whose head-covering cannot be removed so easily.

Jake's ambivalent relationship with traditional dress is soon revealed further in a short but significant scene. Having received notice of his father's death, Jake attempts to mourn according to Jewish tradition. At home, he wears his *tallit* (prayer shawl) and the fashionable new hat which we saw him buy from a market trader. Jake mouths the words of prayer – presumably the *kaddish* verses which are recited after the death a loved one – and soon tearfully gives up. Perhaps he has forgotten the words (as Cahan describes in *Yekl*), or he feels prayer is useless or meaningless, or he is simply overcome with grief. In *Hester Street*, the complex mixture of the former, religious Jake and Jake-in-America is made visible through the combination of the new hat and the traditional *tallit*, which he keeps in his possession. The costume and the ritual go together, but the intention to pray is unrewarding. The *tzitzit* (fringes) on the shawl symbolise a reminder and a physical way to link back to one's roots. We see Jake attempting to connect with his past, but with his father now dead, the gulf of time and place is too great.

The change in Jake's outward appearance is evident from Gitl's reaction upon seeing him for the first time at Ellis Island. One of the first things Gitl says is: 'My God, he's shaved off his beard!' She later tells Jake that she did not recognise him: 'I didn't know you at first, I thought you were a nobleman.' This perception reveals that Gitl interprets the moustache (with no beard) to signify Jake's change of social status, and even ethnicity. Gitl's response suggests her limited frame of reference, as she says this before she has seen anything of America, where men commonly wore moustaches. In Jewish law, there is no requirement for men to grow a beard: it is a matter of custom which varies according to time, place and circumstance.

At certain points of collective and individual mourning, men are not supposed to shave, including for thirty days after the death of a close relative. Jake's choice to wear a moustache indicates adoption of American fashion, and would only signify a breach of Jewish commandment if he was still in the mourning period. The difference in Jake's facial hair symbolises that he, like his beard, is now 'cut off', a concept that I return to later regarding Yossele.

### Gitl's *sheitl* and *tichl*

The Jewish laws of head covering are different for men and for women. Women do not need to cover their heads while saying a blessing but, as we see clearly in *Hester Street*, married women are expected to cover their hair, as are divorcees and widows. As soon as Jake and Gitl are alone together, the disagreement begins over Gitl's head-covering. Once Yossele is put to bed, husband and wife can talk freely. Jake asks how long his father was unwell before he died, and then Gitl wants to embrace. We are shown the differing psychological positions of the couple, as one speaks of death and the other demonstrates desire. Jake's lack of attraction towards Gitl is evident, as he rejects her, saying: 'In America, they don't wear *sheitls*.' Gitl offers to wear her *tichl* (headscarf) rather than *sheitl*, which is also dismissed by Jake: 'They don't wear *tichls* either.' Gitl knows the

rules, and exclaims: 'I can't go around in my own hair, I'm a married woman.' Reluctantly, Jake agrees to the *tichl*.

There are many different rules and traditions among Jewish communities pertaining to women's head covering.[2] Some authorities oblige married women to cover their hair with a wig, scarf or hat, and opinions vary as to how much hair should be covered and how much can be exposed, as well as whether hair should be covered within the house or private locations (with dispute over how to define these spaces). The options depend on community, family and local custom. The requirement stems from a passage in the Torah which describes how to indict a woman suspected of adultery (Numbers 5:11–20): 'And the priest shall stand the woman before God and "*parah*" the woman's head.' The precise meaning of *parah* is contested, meaning either to uncover or dishevel. From this passage, it was understood that married women usually did cover or braid their hair, and rules evolved around mandatory head covering. Generally, Orthodox married women cover their hair in public, but this practice varies greatly. With this knowledge, we can better understand Gitl's reaction to Jake's rejection of her head-covering, as well as the evolution of her opinion during *Hester Street*. Uncovering her head completely would go against her tradition, but would also imply Jake's rejection of Gitl as his wife. To show her natural hair would be, for Gitl, to look like the biblical adulteress, or to return to how she looked before she was married. She tells Jake that she does not want to look like a non-Jewish woman. The head-covering is a sign to the outside world that Gitl is not to be desired by other men. But as the customs vary across communities, Gitl must trust Jake (and later, Mrs Kavarsky) regarding what married Jewish women in America do. In preparation for the role, Carol Kane's acting coach Marilyn Fried encouraged Kane to walk around in public wearing the wig. Kane realised that Gitl would have felt great pride in wearing it, as a symbol of her identity as a married, Jewish woman (Micklin Silver 2021 [2017]).

When Gitl swaps her *sheitl* for a *tichl*, the camerawork conveys the importance of her head-covering. Gitl looks at Jake to signal him to turn away. He walks to the other side of the room, the camera panning to follow him so we cannot see Gitl remove her *sheitl*. The camera cuts back to show Gitl as she wraps a scarf around her head. This sequence marks a key moment of solidarity with Gitl, who does not want to reveal her hair in public (to us). Some Jewish authorities describe women's hair as *ervah* (sexually erotic) and for this reason should be kept from public view. The camera panning away from Gitl in the moment she takes off her wig avoids the voyeurism of a sexualised, male gaze that is dominant in mainstream cinema. Instead, Micklin Silver seems to imbue Gitl's eyes with the power to avert Jake's, and our, gaze. The camerawork supports Gitl's development as a thinking, feeling subject and the horizontal pan refuses to look 'down' on her. The cinematic movement encourages embodied spectatorship, in which we become aware of how our gaze is directed according to Gitl's will, and as a result we gain insight into her frame of mind. This scene is an example of how ways of filming women can present 'a different kind of looking' (Bolton 2011: 196). A close-up draws our gaze to Gitl's pleading but confused eyes, framed by the dark headscarf, and we see her as a young woman who wants to be loved, rather than as a sexual object.

Gitl continues to approach Jake but he rejects her and leaves. The subsequent scene provides a coda. Mr Bernstein tells Gitl that

'Jake's gone out.' Gitl is baffled, not realising that her husband Yankl now has a new, American name – beginning with an unfamiliar 'J' sound that is not used in Yiddish or Hebrew.

## Yossele/Joey

The next scene starts with the sound of Gitl crying out, before we are shown what is happening. We then see Jake grab the kitchen scissors and cut Yossele's *payot* (sidelocks) (pronounced *payes* in Yiddish). Jake admires the new look and calls him 'A little Yankee.' 'Bless him, our little Yossele,' remarks a distraught Gitl, who is again wearing her wig. 'Forget Yossele, from now on, his name is "Joey",' Jake commands.

Long sidelocks, which can be seen more subtly on Shloimy towards the beginning of *Hester Street*, are grown by some observant Jewish men and boys according to the rule for men not to 'round the corners of your head' (Leviticus 19:27). While many Jewish men observe this rule imperceptibly by cutting sideburns no shorter than the 5mm below the cheekbone, others interpret it according to their tradition of growing locks long, or not cutting them at all. In cutting off his son's *payot*, Jake symbolically cuts ties with 'Yossele' and affirms his son's new name. This mirrors Jake's own hair transition from bearded Yankl (ironically sounding like Yankee) in Russia to American Jake with a fashionable moustache. The instances that connect cutting with

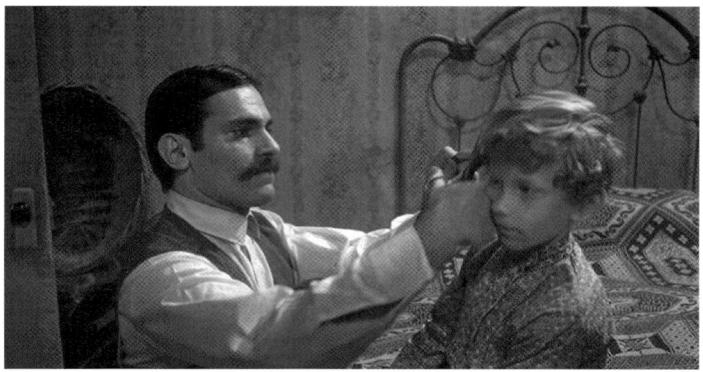

naming subtly echo a Jewish baby boy's *brit milah*, the circumcision ceremony when the child is named. Gitl's horrified reaction to Jake cutting their son's hair is to recourse to superstition, putting salt in Yossele's pockets to avert the evil eye. This superstition has no basis in Jewish law but occurs in many cultures around the world. Feeling helpless, Gitl is doing what little she can to protect her son.

### Gitl's hair

There is significant build-up to Gitl's hair uncovering. She shows her hair as a last resort in trying to make Jake desire her. Gitl welcomes a pedlar (veteran Yiddish performer Leib Lensky) into her home and

with some bashfulness asks for a love potion. Mrs Kavarsky prevents the purchase, resolving to help Gitl herself through practical, rather than superstitious, means.

Gitl allows Mrs Kavarsky to choose new clothes and hats – an idea that has already been suggested by Jake. Although Gitl is reluctant to break religious rules of dress, she would like to try on a hat with feathers, like Mamie's. Gitl accepts Mrs Kavarsky's justification of her own manner of dress as being modest and appropriate for a pious Jewish woman in America: 'We live in an educated country, so we dress like educated people.' Through Gitl's friendship with Mrs Kavarsky, she is learning the *minhag hamakom* and the *dat Yehudit*.

The scene of Gitl's hair-reveal is preceded by a glimpse into Jake's dejected mood, as he and Mr Bernstein have just heard that they will not work for months. Gitl is waiting for Jake in their home, excited to show him her new look, but when he arrives, he is grumbling about work and at first does not look at her. When he does notice her well-arranged, fashionable hairstyle, he immediately gets angry and shouts at her to 'Take it off!' He lunges towards Gitl's head, pulling at her hair. 'It doesn't come off, it's my own hair!' Gitl cries.

Mrs Kavarsky intervenes, chastising Jake and seeking to protect Gitl. Evidently, Gitl's makeover has backfired. However, the rejection

spurs Gitl on her journey of self-determination, as she tells Mrs Kavarsky that she has had 'Enough!' of Jake. The revealing of her real hair signifies the moment when Gitl confirms her independence. Without the wig, Gitl wears no head-covering as marker of marital or religious status or identity. She comes out of her room, her natural hair dishevelled, telling Jake (in Yiddish): 'You and your Polish whore can jump out of your skins!'

## Gitl's clothes

Jake responds to Gitl's new hairstyle and ignores her clothes. The viewer – unlike Jake – has seen the effort that Gitl put into her appearance: we see her try on a corset, hats and clothing, and witness her enjoyment at looking in the mirror. She becomes a viewer of herself, both critical and appreciative. The process of abandoning her dowdy clothes and adjusting her appearance is instrumental in building Gitl's identity, specifically as an American. Film and philosophy theorist Lucy Bolton discussed mirrors within films and the screen-as-mirror to consider how the subjectivity of women might be conveyed in ways that differ from patriarchal, conventional modes of representation (2011: 36). She concluded that:

Perhaps one way to represent something different would be to challenge woman's relationship to the mirror – what she does in front of it, what the mirror does for her, what happens when she applies make-up, how she responds to her reflected image – thereby challenging or interrogating the notion of physical beauty, artifice, and reflection. (Ibid.: 39)

*Hester Street* plays with the trope of the makeover in front of a mirror by presenting the scene from a religious woman's perspective: we do not see Gitl naked or eroticised, she keeps her *sheitl* on underneath her hat, and female friendship is strengthened through

the transformation. Gitl is shown laughing at her reflection when she goes to considerable effort but Jake does not come home; only Mr Bernstein sees her new look. The makeover does not have the desired effect of eliciting her husband's desire. It is not until the close of *Hester Street* that we see Gitl has committed to a new look: to please herself, not Jake.

The makeover is a common feature in mainstream films that are marketed to appeal to young women, encouraging the fantasy that with a little help, any plain girl can become beautiful and sexually attractive. This would, according to generic convention, lead to Gitl achieving her goals and securing her love-interest's attention. In *Hester Street*, the trope is subverted. Gitl does not become more sexually attractive to Jake as intended. Mr Bernstein, on the other hand, was already attracted to Gitl, because of, and not despite, her *tzniut* (modesty).

Gitl's clothing, while often dowdy, does not denote her specifically as Jewish. The stringent Jewish rules pertaining to dress dictate that women should cover their elbows, knees and collarbone, in order to avoid provoking gazes from men other than their husband. According to Orthodox rules, women should take care over their appearance, without drawing attention to themselves. The poor immigrants of the Lower East Side had very few material possessions, and new clothing was a symbol of great luxury, even for those who

worked in the garment trade. To enjoy fashion also meant entering the consumerist culture of America. In New York in the 1890s, the trend for high necklines and long skirts evidently meant that Gitl would not have to compromise her modesty to dress in a contemporary style. As Jake points out, here anyone can dress like Mamie.

## How do I look?

In *Hester Street*, costume and outward appearance reflect the internal, emotional changes that the protagonists experience as they adjust to life in America. Dress, hair and the adoption or rejection of traditions are visible markers of difference between and within the characters. The emphasis on dressing the body, manifested on screen especially through the mirror-makeover scene, connects appearance and looking. Jewish Orthodox law has a lot to say about what women should do to restrict men's view of their bodies, as well as stressing the importance for men to control their own gaze. The sight of Gitl's natural hair does not make her the sexualised object of Jake's gaze, but rather it triggers his violent reaction. In *Hester Street*, we see the narrative power of different kinds of gazes: the looks of disgust and embarrassment (Jake to Gitl), unrequited desire (Gitl to Jake), reciprocated desire (Gitl and Mr Bernstein to each other) and self-appreciation (Gitl's mirror gaze).

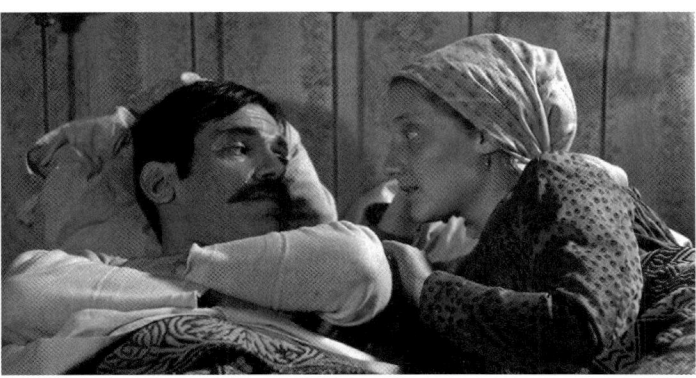

Interestingly, it was Mel Howard's eyes which led to him being cast in the role of Mr Bernstein: he had met Joan Micklin Silver initially for a job as an assistant director on the production. When the original actor dropped out, Micklin Silver said she wanted someone who had eyes like Howard's, and once she learnt that he grew up in a Yiddish-speaking, Lubavitch (a branch of Hasidic Orthodoxy) family, he was cast without hesitation. Through Mr Bernstein's gaze, we realise that Gitl is the object of his desire, as he admires her in ways that Jake does not.

In Jewish religious life and in cinema, dressing faces, hair and clothing is significant and deliberate. There are parallels between clothing and costume, and ritual and performance, as processes which reflect psychological states, beliefs and group identification. In both religion and cinema, the meaning of outward appearance involves responding to codes which are recognised and interpreted differently depending on the viewer's knowledge and understanding (Hall 1993).

Gitl's changing appearance is a manifestation of her faltering, experimental journey of identity as an American Jewish woman. Through insights into the emotional lives of the characters in *Hester Street*, audiences are encouraged not to judge religious people by their appearance, but rather to consider the individual behind the costume.

# 5 Money, Freedom, Knowledge – and Desire

The Jews who wanted to be one hundred percent cosmopolitan switched to other cultures and grew accustomed to foreign languages. Those drawn to Yiddish words, to Yiddish letters, were bound by a thousand threads to the whole spiritual baggage of the Diaspora. This is especially the case in a free country like America, where no political or economic pressures force the Jew into cultural isolation. If he willingly separates himself, he does so not for 'worldly' reasons, but because of his need to identify with Judaism and Jewish values. (Singer 1989 [1943]: 10)

Isaac Bashevis Singer, writing in New York in Yiddish for *Svive* (*Surroundings*) journal in 1943, described the tensions associated with Yiddish language and culture in cosmopolitan America. The freedom afforded to Jews in America contrasted with their restricted existence in Europe. America provided new horizons for different expressions of Jewish culture. How can 'spiritual baggage' from deep-rooted communities be carried across transatlantic borders, and how can 'Judaism and Jewish values' inform new identities for immigrants? The characters in *Hester Street* embody different directions of choice. Jake, Mamie, Mr Bernstein, Mrs Kavarsky and Gitl 'switch' or 'separate' as they form American Jewish identities, motivated variously by money, freedom, knowledge and desire.

Nancy drew attention to the performance of identity in accented films: 'Like exile itself, the journey of identity in accented films is processual and endless. Such a journey can also take the form of the performance of identity, whereby exilic subjects travel strategically across a range of identities' (2001: 238). In *Hester Street*, we see how journeys of identities are 'processual' (in movement rather than isolated events) and 'endless' as the characters come up against new challenges and opportunities which force them to adjust continually as newly American Jews. Micklin Silver summed this up, saying, 'the troubles you have as an immigrant don't end when you get off the boat' (2021 [2017]).

## Jake

From the opening scenes that depict Jake and Mamie dancing, they are associated with freedom, fun, youth and sensuality. Jake's motivation to 'switch' cultures is clear. In his view, this means shedding all external signs of Jewishness: hairstyle, clothing, religious observance and language, including names. He plays baseball and sits with a boxing poster next to his workstation, proclaiming himself to be 'a regular Yankee'. Despite Jake's move away from religious observance and Yiddish speech, there is no indication that he wants to leave the Lower East Side or the Jewish community. His personal struggles stem from his ambivalence and tension between his old and new ways of life. Gitl and Yossele's arrival puts into relief both how far Jake has come in his three years in America, and yet how closely he is bound to his past. Jake's life, like his speech, is accented. We meet Jake mid-journey in the transitional space of the Lower East Side.

Jake admires Mamie for her modern outlook. When Joe Peltner confides in Jake that he intends to ask Mamie to marry him, Jake tries

to dissuade him by extolling Gitl's virtues: 'When I finish work and I come home all I want to do is eat my dinner, enjoy my little wife and play with my boychik.' Jake tells Joe that 'American ladies are good for fun' – here describing Mamie as 'American' because to him, she represents everything American despite her Polish background, or possibly precisely because of her ability to adjust. Women from 'the home country', according to Jake, clean the house and don't ask for anything: he means women who do not assimilate. In reality, *shtetl* (village) women were hard workers who often supported their husbands financially (Stahl Weinberg 1988). It is during this conversation that Joe also tells Jake that Mamie has saved more than $300 from her wages, with which she intends to open a dance academy. This is key information that Jake feigns not to know later in the film.

Jake lies, keeps secrets and visits a prostitute. He manipulates Mamie into lending him money, leading her to believe that he intends to propose to her. Until his family's arrival, Jake has told no one that he is married with a child, yet when Mr Bernstein asks, 'For whom is the little bed?', Jake retorts: 'Did I ever say I was a single man?' Jake's behaviour discourages audience sympathy. Yet, as Mr Bernstein tells Gitl when she expresses concern that Jake no longer loves her, Jake

'A Gallery of Missing Husbands', *Forward*, 9 June 1912

is not the worst of men: 'He sent for you, didn't he? There are men who abandon their wives, too.' Indeed, abandonment was a problem for many families during this period. Husbands went missing due to the pressures of responsibility, the lure of 'too much' freedom and the possibility of a new life of anonymity in such a vast country – a factor suggested when Jake says there is 'no such thing as relatives' in America. The issue was widespread enough that *Forward* printed 'A Gallery of Missing Husbands' on its back page every Sunday from 1908 to 1920, encouraging American and international readers to reconnect missing people to their families. The text beneath the headline reads: 'If you recognize them and know where they are, let their wives know through *Forward*.'[3] Unlike the missing husbands, Jake barely travels beyond Hester Street. His character does not develop significantly, but he has travelled 'across a range of identities' before the period that *Hester Street* depicts: we perceive his change through Gitl's reactions.

After attacking Gitl and realising that she knows about his relationship with Mamie, Jake expresses his conflicted feelings to Mrs Kavarsky: 'I don't care for no dancing girls! I don't care for nobody! Especially that one, that *schnoozer*.[4] I'm an American fella, I'm a Yankee, that's what I am, and that's all. Ah, it's no use!'

Jake 'wanted to be one hundred percent cosmopolitan' but his pursuit of freedom and independence is ultimately 'no use!' By the end of *Hester Street*, Jake has neither money nor freedom. Immediately following his divorce from Gitl, he will marry Mamie and must return to the sweatshop. Jake is not 'bound by a thousand threads', but he is hanging on by some threads that he cannot sever.

## Mamie

Mamie is hard-working, determined, romantic and hopeful – although a fool in love. Her character is more fleshed out in *Hester Street* than in *Yekl*. In the film, she values money and her name hints at linguistic connotations: Mamie/money, Fein/fine. In the early café scene, Mamie explains that she wants to have her own money by the time she marries: 'I don't want somebody to say they had to take me, even though she's poor, just as she is.' For Mamie, having money will lessen pity and increase respect. She implies that everything she now has, she has earned herself on American soil.

Mamie loans Jake $25 for furniture, presuming that he will soon propose marriage: romance and money are bound up together for her. Sometime later, she goes to Jake's home to chase the loan and to see Jake. Here, Mamie and Gitl come face to face, maintaining their composure as it dawns on them that they have both been deceived.

Mamie asks Yossele for a kiss and gives him a coin in exchange: a mirror of her relationship with Jake (and an exchange which Micklin Silver recalled her Yiddish-speaking grandmother making). Gitl apprehensively welcomes Mamie in Yiddish, saying, 'Why should you stand, you may be seated for the same money', a common Yiddish phrase, perhaps, but apt considering Mamie's associations with money. Jake becomes increasingly agitated, ordering Gitl to put their son to bed. Mamie takes the opportunity to make herself heard, in a conversation with Jake that links money with knowledge:

MAMIE      I don't know where you give it to, a married man, with a darling little wife. I must remember to ask your wife how she likes the furniture. The furniture you bought with my money.

JAKE      I'll pay you every penny, Mamie. Just don't say nothing to her, please.

MAMIE      What do I care, I want my money! I worked hard enough for it. I'll say what I like to your wife. Oh, don't you like it? Lump it!

JAKE      Don't talk English, she will think something.

MAMIE      I do not care what she thinks. I want she should know.

A later scene shows Jake and Mamie kissing on a rooftop before discussing the possibility of Jake and Gitl's divorce:

JAKE      Mamie, how can you fix? She don't want agree to a divorce.
MAMIE      Money, money, money.
JAKE      I ain't got.
MAMIE      I got.
JAKE      *You* got?
MAMIE      You knew I got, ain't you?
JAKE      Never! How much you got?
MAMIE      $340!

[Kissing]

It used to be $365 but for the $25 you borrowed, I already said *kaddish*. Ach, we'll keep by enough to start a dancing academy. We're done with the sweatshops, Jake.

Unlike Mamie, we know that Joe Peltner already told Jake about the savings. Mamie shares money on condition of Jake's devotion. Her attitude can be compared with Jake's unromantic, transactional behaviour towards money and sex, evident from his visit to a prostitute as well as his manipulation of Mamie. Ultimately, Mamie does not seem to resent paying the divorce settlement, accepting the deal with good humour. Only on Gitl's arrival in America does Mamie become 'the other woman' and she is not depicted as a classical homewrecker or temptress (Berke 2021).

## Mrs Kavarsky and Mr Bernstein

Mrs Kavarsky is a stereotypical local busybody, dropping in at her neighbours' homes and proffering advice. Her English speech conveys the flavour of wise Yiddish idiom, her sharp tongue delivering the best zingers. She tells Jake: 'With one *tuchus* [backside] you can't dance at two weddings', and 'You can't pee up my back and make me think it's rain' – phrases which actress Doris Roberts suggested for inclusion, remembering her grandfather saying them in Yiddish. Mrs Kavarsky commands respect from Jake, telling him that 'I was already in America when you were still blowing the bellows in Russia', reflecting how the pecking order in the Lower East Side

depended on how long someone had been in the country. Gitl leans on Mrs Kavarsky as her respected advisor. Mrs Kavarsky has made her choices and settled into Jewish American life, without seeming conflicted in her identity.

Mr Bernstein is introduced early in *Hester Street*, as a co-worker of Jake's in the sweatshop. The camera pans around a small room in which at least six people are working, including a child, as was customary. One of the workers was played by a representative from the International Ladies Garment Workers Union, on set to provide the authentic sewing machines and supervise their operation (Micklin Silver and Silver 2021 [2004]). The boss (Martin Garner) teases his employees:

BOSS             Bernstein, what was you in the old country? A *yeshiva*
                 [Jewish school] student? Sitting on your *tuchus* all day in
                 the study house? Hahaha. And the women is bringing
                 the food for the scholar, and everyone is fighting, 'Stay in
                 my house, stay by me.' And, 'Please, do me the honour to
                 marry with my daughter.' Huh, well, I wasn't no boss in
                 Lithuania, no sir, give a guess what I was?

MR BERNSTEIN     A pedlar

BOSS            Huh, I told you already? Some country, America, huh? The
pedlar becomes the boss, and the *yeshiva bocher* [student]
sits by the sewing machine. Some country, huh Jake?'

Mr Bernstein responds with his characteristic calm resolve. The
boss resembles an unsympathetic Jewish stereotype, whose presence
indicates the labour exploitation and difficulties of Lower East Side
life, even within Jewish communities. The boss's speech provides one
of the film's few descriptions of life 'in the old country', and reveals
Mr Bernstein's social predicament as well as his strength of character.
The placement of this scene near the beginning of the film sets up the
possibility of social mobility and reversal of fortune, in which the
respected become lowly and vice versa. *Hester Street* presents this
inversion with irony, however, as we see that despite differences of
status within the group, the boss has not risen to high rank in terms
of wider American society: the prospects of many new immigrants
remained relatively low.

    Mr Bernstein is willingly tied to the 'spiritual baggage' of
Yiddish culture and Jewish observance. He does not separate himself
completely from the American world in which he lives, proving to
be a good English speaker while also pursuing religious learning and
observance. The ways in which Mr Bernstein is filmed emphasise his

piety, gentleness and desire. In a heartfelt conversation, he tells Gitl
about his motivations for coming to America, explaining that he
could not concentrate on his studies. The characters are positioned in
such a way as to avoid direct eye contact, both facing the camera:

I wasn't worthy. I could not take my mind off profanities. Even when I was
studying the Talmud. It teaches, 'he who even looks at the little finger of a
woman is as guilty as though he looks at a woman totally naked.' So, I bought
a ship's ticket and I came to America.

Gitl's astonished expression emphasises the eroticism and potential
transgressiveness of his confession. They laugh together at the difficulty
of being religiously observant Jews in the US, repeating 'a curse on
Columbus!', a common Yiddish phrase that expressed 'the anger of
disillusionment' with the *goldene medina* (Goldsmith 1979: 48).

Gitl confides in Mr Bernstein and asks him about Mamie. Mr
Bernstein is lit with the soft glow of the table lamp as he leans over
the religious texts he is studying. His pale hands stretch across the
table's mid-point, a line which is suggestive of a *mechitza*, a partition
between men and women. Mr Bernstein dares to touch Gitl's shawl
after she has drawn her hands away from his, in a gesture that shows

that sexual attraction and romantic love can be expressed very differently from Jake's passionate groping of Mamie. This was an improvised gesture that caught Micklin Silver's eye during a break in filming, and she realised that the fondling perfectly communicated the affection and tension that she was attempting to convey in this scene (Micklin Silver and Silver 2021 [2004]).

Sam Posner in *Crossing Delancey* (1988)

Mr Bernstein is ridiculed by Jake for his 'greenhorn' ways and yet, it is Mr Bernstein who is more knowledgeable than Jake. He is quietly self-assured, teaches Yossele Hebrew, and proves himself to be kind and generous. Mr Bernstein's character is similar to that of Sam Posner (Peter Riegert), the pickle seller and 'nice Jewish man' who is the romantic hero of *Crossing Delancey*.

Mr Bernstein gets the last laugh, after Jake's relentless

teasing about finding a wife. At the end of *Hester Street*, Mr Bernstein walks with Jake's ex-wife and son to his former home, eliciting audience satisfaction at the ironic outcome.

## Gitl

In Cahan's *Yekl*, Gitl is stout and dark, a stereotypical hysterical woman, prone to outbursts of sobbing, tears and fainting swoons. In contrast, Micklin Silver recreates Gitl as the heroine of *Hester Street*. The director identified strongly with Gitl:

> When I was adapting the screenplay and directing the movie, I saw there was a parallel between Gitl's story and my story. She wanted to succeed in America without losing a sense of herself and where she came from, and I wanted to succeed as a director without losing a sense of myself as a woman, the kind of person I was. So I constantly thought of that as we went along.
>
> (Micklin Silver and Silver 2021 [2004])

The viewer is encouraged to identify with Gitl through insights into her inner thoughts and feelings, effected with cinematic perspective, camerawork, editing and plot. Micklin Silver wills Gitl, and herself, to succeed.

Gitl arrives in America with a predefined role, as Jake announces: 'For the purpose that she is my wife.' She knows no one in New York apart from Jake. We are invited to feel sorry for her when deserted by Jake on her first night, and when she says that she has barely left the apartment. Gitl's isolation conforms to Naficy's observation that 'sadness, loneliness, and alienation are frequent themes' of accented cinema (2001: 27). Gitl's loneliness, however, is short-lived, as she bonds with both Mrs Kavarsky and Mr Bernstein.

Gitl reluctantly adapts her outward appearance, yet she is not prepared to compromise on her marital, sexual needs. Gitl desires and expects intimacy from Jake, frequently instigating their physical relationship. She even confides in Mr Bernstein that she wants her sex life to be as it was in the past. For much of the film, Gitl's motivation

is to restore Jake's attraction towards her, but she must negotiate how much she is willing to change for him. Gitl is effectively becoming reshaped in America according to her own choices. Lucy Bolton's discussion of how films construct 'thinking women' described the lead character of *In the Cut* (dir. Jane Campion, 2003) as 'a woman who is "becoming"' (2011: 94), a description that could also apply to Gitl. *Hester Street* conveys Gitl's inner life most strikingly through Carol Kane's eyes. When she sees Mr Bernstein washing his hands before blessing bread (according to Jewish law)

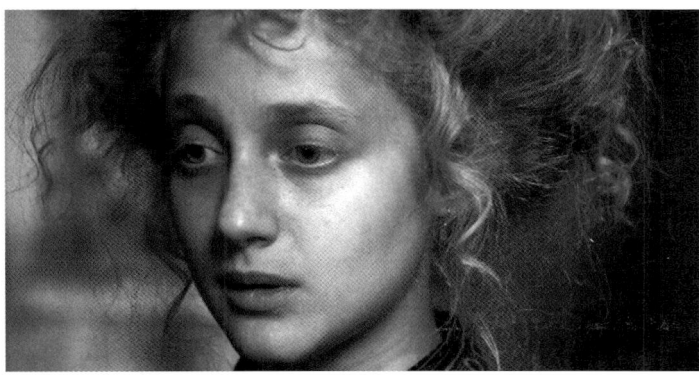

and eating the meal that she has prepared, Gitl's eyes flicker in acknowledgement at the contrast between his piety and her husband's boorishness; the possibility of her desire is communicated in a small, silent gesture. Kane's performance effectively embodies Gitl's character growth. As perceived in a 1975 review in the *New York Times*, 'Miss Kane manages the high acting feat of seeming to change size physically, expanding and shrinking as she is happy or miserable' (Eder 1975: 44).

Mamie's lawyer tries to persuade Gitl to agree to a divorce. At a meeting in her home, Gitl wears dark clothes and a black *tichl*. Her pale face is framed like a renaissance portrait. Kane's ability to communicate both softness and strength is evident. When the lawyer offers increasing sums of money, Gitl does not respond with speech but with her gaze. Eventually, she goes to the window, turns sideways and glares at the lawyer over her shoulder. A classical shot/reverse-shot sequence narrates a conversation, although Gitl converses only through her eyes, her strongest expressive tool. Gitl opts out of communication in a language she struggles to speak. The director used a technique she learnt as a journalist when interviewing: that if you are quiet, the other person will keep talking just to fill the silence (Micklin Silver 2021 [2017]). Carol Kane reflected on the scene:

I don't say anything for the whole scene, and the lawyer misinterprets me not saying anything, so he just offers me more and more money. I end up with all the money, and that wasn't my character's intent. I'm just so appalled and devastated that he [Jake] would have done that – that he would have sent this man to me. It was like a silent-movie moment. I really love that. The less talking the better, as far as I'm concerned. (quoted in Ebiri 2021)

From Kane's description, we can better understand that Gitl is refusing or unable to enter into the negotiation. *Hester Street* provides a 'space of consciousness' (Bolton 2011: 75) in which the viewer becomes increasingly aware of Gitl's feelings, with emphasis on her thought and gaze. Micklin Silver foregrounds Gitl's interiority,

countering the dominant filmic language that privileges speech and action, and objectifies the female body. The performance, cinematography and editing support reading the scene as an example of what film theorist Mary Ann Doane described as '"speaking" the female body differently, even haltingly or inarticulately from the perspective of a classical syntax' (1991: 176).

The scene ends before we know if Gitl and the lawyer have reached an agreement. The significance of the gaze is strengthened by the subsequent scene, in which Gitl comes out of her bedroom

wearing new clothes. She asks, 'Mr Bernstein, is alright these things?
Mrs Kavarsky says for a divorce a woman must not look like an
old woman.' Gitl invites Mr Bernstein to turn his gaze towards her.
Micklin Silver invests Gitl with the ability to control how she is
looked at, and by whom.

Gitl is surprised to find Mr Bernstein packing up his books. He
explains that he cannot afford to pay his board and asks Gitl to say
goodbye to Yossele from him:

| | |
|---|---|
| GITL | May you have a boy of your own one day. |
| MR BERNSTEIN | From your mouth to God's ear [in Yiddish]. To have a son, one must have a wife. |
| GITL | A wife you can get. |
| MR BERNSTEIN | The one that I would ask, what if she would say no? |
| GITL | What if she would say yes? |
| [Cutting the string that ties his books] | |
| MR BERNSTEIN | Mrs, what are you doing? |
| GITL | I'm saying yes. |
| MR BERNSTEIN | Thank you. |
| GITL | You're welcome. |

Gitl and Mr Bernstein touch hands and with that, they are engaged.
The scene exudes sweetness and gentleness, in contrast to the
turbulence of Jake and Gitl's strained relationship, and Jake and
Mamie's physical passion.

Gitl expresses her love for Mr Bernstein by welcoming the very
books which Jake ridiculed. The cutting of the string (which Gitl
has just given to Mr Bernstein) symbolises her desire to prevent him
from leaving, and her acceptance of his most precious belongings
– his books, now rooted in the apartment. Singer's metaphorical
language is materialised: Mr Bernstein is 'bound by a thousand
threads to the whole spiritual baggage of the Diaspora', the threads
are his string; the 'spiritual baggage' is his books, a portable link to
centuries of tradition. Gitl and Mr Bernstein are now mostly speaking

in English to one another. They are both adapting to American life while upholding religious practice. As Singer observed: 'If he willingly separates himself, he does so not for "worldly" reasons, but because of his need to identify with Judaism and Jewish values.' Mr Bernstein and Gitl identify each other with Judaism and Jewish values: they willingly separate themselves, together.

### Free will? The divorce

The solemn divorce scene towards the end of the film brings together themes of Jewish ritual, sexual inequality and freedom. An Orthodox Jewish divorce can only occur with the issue of a *get* (divorce contract), granted by a husband. The scene takes place in a rabbi's house, before three witnesses, a scribe and the rabbi's wife, who administers the payments. Jake arrives alone and has to borrow a *yarmulke* head-covering, whereas Gitl is accompanied by Mrs Kavarsky and instinctively touches a kiss to the *mezuzah* (a doorpost scroll traditionally kissed on entering and leaving a room). She now wears fashionable clothes, her natural hair adorned with a stylish hat. Jake watches Gitl tentatively, perhaps regretting his rejection of her, while she tries to avert her eyes from him. The proceedings take place in Yiddish, English and Aramaic. A tone of

respectful sadness is created through slow camera movement, no
musical soundtrack and the explicit directions given by the old rabbi,
whom everyone obeys.

   Although some Orthodox women are refused permission to
divorce and remain *agunot* (chained women, unable to remarry),
*Hester Street* highlights Gitl's choice:

RABBI   Young woman, here is the writ of divorce. Now you may still
        change your mind. You must accept the divorce with the same
        free will with which you married your husband. Should you have
        the slightest objection in your heart, the divorce is null and void.
        Do you understand?

GITL    Ya

RABBI   Witnesses, hear what this woman says. She accepts this divorce
        with her own free will.

The suggestion of equality is soon countered by the rabbi's pronouncement that: 'Remember, daughter, you may not marry again before ninety-one days. You young man, may wed even today if you agree.' This law may seem unfair, but in fact it serves to avoid questions of paternity arising from pregnancy occurring soon after a divorce. The scene culminates with the rabbi's wife asking the son's name. Mrs Kavarsky says 'Yossele'. But Gitl asserts, 'His name is Joey.' This is a definitive statement of Gitl's Americanisation, on her own terms. She is a person in the process of 'becoming', whose evolution is just starting. Her relative youth and forthcoming marriage to Mr Bernstein suggest her future, rather than a conclusion. Gitl is like the protagonists that Bolton described: 'left with the ambiguous prospects of uncertain futures, but a confidence that those futures can be of their own making' (2011: 175).

### Futures

The final scene opens with Jake and Mamie, who wears a veil and carries a bouquet, walking down Hester Street. Mamie tells Jake that he will have to go back to his job in the sweatshop, but Jake still hopes to start their dancing academy. Mamie sets him straight: 'With what, your wife skinned us alive out of $300, didn't she? We'll have to

start saving all over again, from the very beginning.' This conversation reveals the punchline of *Hester Street*: Gitl received almost all of Mamie's savings, equivalent to over $10,000 today. Gitl's gain and the delay in its revelation adds to the audience's enjoyment. The comment that they will start saving 'from the very beginning' recalls the sweatshop boss's earlier invocation of a possible reversal of fortunes. Gitl and Mr Bernstein then enter the street with Joey (no longer Yossele), discussing their plans to open a grocery store, which Gitl will manage while Mr Bernstein will sit at the back and study – just as Jake suggested in jest (with a different wife in mind). Gitl will save Mr Bernstein from the sweatshop, to which Jake must return.

Much of the viewer's pleasure derives from the disruption of traditional power dynamics that plays out. Mamie and Gitl are not shown arguing with each other, and in this way *Hester Street* avoids the often-represented love triangle fantasy of two women fighting over one man. The film challenges the dominant social order, as cash-strapped Jake is effectively exchanged between Mamie and Gitl. Feminist theorist Luce Irigaray perceived that in capitalist society, 'In order for a product – a woman? – to have value, two men, at least, have to invest (in) her' (1985: 181). In essence, she argued, '[t]he circulation of women among men is what establishes the operations of society, at least of patriarchal society' (ibid.: 184). *Hester Street* inverts this social structure when the money is paid from Mamie to Gitl, rendering Jake the 'product' exchanged between the two women. Although Jake and Mr Bernstein benefit by gaining new wives, it is Mamie and Gitl who exchange money, and Gitl who will invest it in her new business. It is implied that soon Gitl, like Mamie, will be a hard-working, earning woman, reflecting qualities that Jewish culture traditionally holds in high regard.[5]

Gitl arrived as chattel and emerges at the end of *Hester Street* as a romantically fulfilled, prospective business owner. Gitl adapts a little, has gained knowledge about how to navigate her new society, and she retains her Jewish identity and religious observance. Yiddish scholar Miriam Borden observed that Gitl is the most typically American of the characters, for she succeeds where Jake fails in navigating complex identities as Jewish Americans (Reed-Wood 2022).

The ending of *Hester Street* sees Jake and Mamie, and Gitl and Mr Bernstein with Joey, walk off in different literal and metaphorical directions. *Hester Street* links the past with the time of film-making through Joey, who represents the generation of Micklin Silver's parents. The child's presence propels the historical story into an era of living memory, encouraging reflection on how much has changed, and how much is ever the same.

## **6** Situating *Hester Street*

'"Who wants to watch a film about Jews?" As it turns out, everyone!'
(Micklin Silver 2024)

In the fifty years since its initial release, *Hester Street* has been
screened regularly in cinemas, on American broadcast television, in
educational settings, and has been released on multiple home cinema
formats. In 2011, it was included in the National Film Registry of
the US Library of Congress, which selects twenty-five films each year
that are deemed 'culturally, historically or aesthetically significant'
(Library of Congress 2011). Since 2016, the Cohen Media Group has
restored and re-released several films directed by Joan Micklin Silver.
And in April 2024, a stage-play adaptation of *Hester Street* premiered
in Washington, DC. The impact of *Hester Street* and its status as a
classic can be assessed by considering its initial box-office success,
critic reviews, audience response and academic reception.

*Hester Street* had its American theatrical premiere on
19 October 1975 at the Plaza cinema in New York. Joan and
Raphael's daughter Dina Micklin Silver said:

I remember when the film was finally released in theaters. It was pouring
rain. Our parents were so worried, afraid no one would want to go out in such
weather. But when they arrived at the theater for the first showing, there
was actually a line around the block – everyone braving the downpour to see
*Hester Street*. (2024)

*Hester Street* was a hit with audiences in New York and Los
Angeles, and its first short run was extended through the winter into
1976. Non-theatrical sales were also high, as the film was popular on
university campuses and Jewish community centres across America

(Deutchman 2024). As well as an Academy Award nomination for Carol Kane, Joan Micklin Silver was nominated by the Writers Guild of America for Best Comedy Adapted from Another Medium (1976). A downside to the film's success was that Carol Kane was not engaged for more acting work for a year after *Hester Street*, as her performance had been so esoteric (Ryzik 2024).

## Critic reviews

Press reviews on the release of *Hester Street* were, on the whole, positive. Praise for the set design and acting were frequent, although the film also received backhanded compliments, such as in Richard Eder's review in the *New York Times*, which proffered 'there is nothing very original about *Hester Street* except its loveliness' (1975: 44). *Los Angeles Times* critic Charles Champlin was an early advocate, calling the film 'totally beguiling', and he observed that the characters 'don't simply appear, they evolve' (1975: 525) – a feature that I have emphasised in this book.

*Hester Street* failed to win over some critics. Walter Goodman, under the headline 'Overpraised and Overdone' in the *New York Times*, conceded the film was 'by no means without its rewards', but criticised the acting and dialogue (1975: 151). Pauline Kael, known for her biting observations in the *New Yorker*, offered a thoughtful analysis which recognised the commercial appeal of *Hester Street*, but expressed little personal enthusiasm for the film. However, Kael did admit that 'Mel Howard manages to make stillness rather sexy', and concluded that 'Joan Silver may not have a very large talent (at least, in this first feature there's no evidence of shattering vitality), but she *is* gifted' (1975: 167).

*Jump Cut* published a critique in 1976 that focused on *Hester Street*'s lack of analysis of social and economic conditions, pointing out how the film ignored the underlying capitalist expansion and labour exploitation into which the characters were bound (Friedman and Steinberg 1976). Sonya Michel's 1977 article in *Literature/Film Quarterly* compared *Hester Street* with Cahan's text, but provided

Poster designed by Peter Strausfeld, 1975

little close analysis of the film. Michel wrote that Micklin Silver's directing 'underscores a sense of female solidarity' (1977: 144), yet did not elaborate on how the directing operates to this effect.

*Hester Street* premiered in London in October 1975 and screened across the UK through the following year. The reception from British critics was generally positive but revealed both interesting and troubling perspectives on American Jewish life, particularly regarding women. For example, Richard Barkley writing in the *Sunday Express* felt that 'there is a sly woman's touch to the ending' (1975: 22). David Castell lauded *Hester Street* in the *Sunday Telegraph* as 'the most impressive film of the week'. However, he revealed some prejudicial attitudes towards women and Jewish people: 'Although centre screen is occupied by Jake (Steven Keats), a proud new citizen of the States, the story is really of two women, two archetypes of the matriarchy America was to become', and he described Mamie as having 'sloughed off her orthodoxy like a snake does an old skin' (1975: 16). Castell's observation that America was a matriarchy in 1975 is a curious one, especially considering the position of women in the film industry and in wider culture. His comments about Mamie's Orthodoxy (which is not specified in the film) are presumptuous, and furthermore, the age-old comparison of Jewish people to snakes is deeply offensive and antisemitic.

A review by Russell Davies in the *Observer* abounded with negative stereotyping of both women and Jewish people, calling Mamie 'a flashy but shrewd woman of means' and commenting that:

A woman director is a rarity, and one who can muster such beautifully judged recreations of past scenes is more treasurable than most. She has perhaps not quite thought through the consequences of what she is showing here (the woman takes charge, fine, but one wants to know of what: just another hard-headed business empire ruled with peasant cunning?). (1975: 28)

The *Guardian*'s highly regarded film critic Derek Malcolm described Gitl's *sheitl* as 'a Jewish peasant's wig' and wrote that Jake's 'mistress exhibits some of the old world's propensity for shrewd bargaining' (1975: 8). Likewise, Arthur Thirkell called Gitl 'shrewd' in the *Daily Mirror* (1975: 23). The foreignness of the characters depicted in *Hester Street* was emphasised, for instance by Eric Shorter in the *Daily Telegraph*, who enjoyed the film, yet pointed out that 'every now and then it lapses into Yiddish or whatever it was that the immigrants were apt to lapse into' (1975: 13). Shorter's flippancy is dismissive and condescending, creating a distance between the culture depicted and the presumed cultural background of his readership.

Many of these British reviewers enjoyed *Hester Street*, and yet the antisemitic descriptors such as 'flashy', 'shrewd', 'hard-headed business empire', 'peasant', 'cunning', 'sly' and snake-like reveal then prevalent attitudes towards Jewish people. The interpretations contrast with Carol Kane's understanding of Gitl being 'appalled and devastated' at the divorce (Ebiri 2021), and the critics' comments often reinforce negative stereotypes of Jewish people as duplicitous, eternally 'other', greedy and hiding deviously within dominant culture. They dissuade audiences from perceiving the pride in Jewish culture and Gitl's growth, which lie at the heart of the film. When describing Gitl and Mamie, we must also question how much sexism plays a part. Indeed, Shorter felt rather sorry for 'well-intentioned' Jake. The *Jewish Chronicle*'s female reviewer, perhaps unsurprisingly, praised *Hester Street* and valued the film's rare positive portrayal of Jewish people (Melnikoff 1976: 10).

The contrasting reception in the American and British press in the 1970s can be understood, to a degree, by differences in the Jewish communities. The UK has a much smaller Jewish population, both in number and proportion of total population; there are, and were, relatively fewer Jewish film critics in the UK. New York and Los Angeles are centres of Jewish American life as well as being the bases for national media outlets, potentially accounting for the higher proportion of film critics who may have been sensitive to Jewish readership. Significantly, the cultural environment in the 1970s that encouraged the exploration of roots and cultural identity did not take as strong a hold in the UK for British Jews, who tended to be more reluctant to stand out as different or sought to blend in with wider British culture – no doubt in reaction to widespread prejudice. There were few overt depictions of Jewish life in British film and television. Jack Rosenthal's 1976 television play *Bar Mitzvah Boy* was the first of its kind to put British Jewish life in the mainstream public sphere – yet this sharp comedy did little to dispel stereotypes of Jewish women as brash and hysterical (Wagner 2022).

*Hester Street* earned an important place in the public imagination partly because its depictions of immigration and the American dream were common to many people, regardless of country of origin. It is an example of accented cinema's wide appeal. The film struck a chord with audiences just at the time when interest in immigration stories was high, especially in the US (Diner 2000, 2011).

Throughout the 1980s and 1990s, *Hester Street* continued to be screened internationally. Mark Balsam, distributor of the film through Westchester Films from the late 1970s until the 2010s, stated that 'Hester Street had a very, very meaningful and longstanding cachet. It did for years' (2024). An interview with German-born, Jewish film-maker Liliane Targownik (born 1959) is illustrative of the film's impact in post-Holocaust Europe:

The first film about Jewish life that I saw was Hester Street by Joan Micklin Silver. I remember seeing it in Munich with my family and other people from the Jewish community. Everybody was very moved and proud that there was a film about us. There were only 5,000 Jews in Munich out of a total population of 1.5 million. (Baron and Targownik 2003: 117–18)

## Jewish studies

Hester Street has received most scholarly attention from within Jewish studies, but even this is minimal. From the 1980s, academics increasingly looked back on the history of Jewish representation on screen and behind the scenes in Hollywood. An emphasis on mainstream, studio-produced cinema meant that Hester Street was at times overlooked, although the popularity of the film, and Joan Micklin Silver's later success with Crossing Delancey, drew some comment.

Patricia Erens' 1984 volume, The Jew in American Cinema, lists significant portrayals of Jewish characters comprehensively but offers little in-depth analysis. Erens claimed that '[o]f all the films produced in the seventies, the most unique female portrait is in Joan Micklin Silver's Hester Street' (1984: 325). By contrast, Lester Friedman called Hester Street 'an overly sentimental adaptation' (1987: 209). His opinion seems to hinge upon his dislike – and, I would argue, misinterpretation – of the characters and plot; for example, he felt that Gitl 'fails to accomplish much worthwhile' (ibid.: 210). Friedman's response to Hester Street is representative of a view that dismisses the film's contribution to the history of Jewish and/or women's film-making, and undervalues its popularity.

Overviews of Jewish American cinema tend to sweep past Micklin Silver.[6] Despite seeking to provide a comprehensive historical account, Joel Rosenberg briefly mentioned *Hester Street*, misspelling the director as 'Mecklin' and focusing on other film-makers instead (1996). Here, as in many other studies,[7] Barbra Streisand received more attention, although Helene Meyers did assert that Micklin Silver 'should be as well-known as Babs' (2021: 74).

Carol Kane as Gitl features on the cover of *The Jewish-American Stage and Screen: From Hester Street to Hollywood* (Blacher Cohen 1986), but only a few words about the film are included in the book's pages. The reference to Hester Street as a geographical place in the title and Gitl's cover image reinforce the symbolic power of *Hester Street* in American public imagination and memory.

Sonya Michel acknowledged that there was little incorporation (in the 1990s) of feminist theory and gender studies into scholarship of Jewish film, and she sought to bring these perspectives together. From this promising intention, Michel gave *Hester Street* just a nod, pointing out that it adapts Cahan's story with 'a feminist gloss' (1994: 258).

Social and cultural historian Joyce Antler has written extensively about portrayals of Jewish women in the media (1998, 2007). Discussing *Hester Street* in *Past Imperfect*, Antler focused on historical analysis and interpreted its depictions of gender relations sympathetically:

*Hester Street* succeeds in portraying the inexorable process of assimilation, while suggesting that it affects males and females differently. Refusing to blame women for progressing too rapidly (like Mamie) or too slowly (like Gitl), the film implies that these women will have a powerful hand in determining their families' American futures; in both the story and the film, it is Jake who is ultimately more bewildered than either Gitl or Mamie. In indicating the hardships experienced by women and their resiliency, as well as the deep strains assimilation posed to masculinity, *Hester Street* touches on a fundamental cultural challenge confronting immigrants. (1995: 181)

Vincent Brook proposed the term 'Jew Wave' in recognition of the Jewish contribution to New Hollywood between 1967 and 1980 (2019), and yet rather than evaluating Joan Micklin Silver's work, he only mentions *Hester Street* in a concluding list of films for future consideration. A few other studies have given more attention to *Hester Street*. Stephen Whitfield considered the film in terms of its depiction of nineteenth-century America (2019) and Hasia Diner (2000, 2011) contextualised it as an example of American cultural concern with ethnicity and identity in the 1970s. Lawrence Baron acknowledged Micklin Silver as one of 'The Pioneering American Jewish Women Directors', and his assessment of *Hester Street* rejected Friedman's 1987 scathing interpretation (Baron 2021). Hammerman studied the film in terms of adaptation and Jewish religious clothing (2018), yet, as I noted in Chapter 5, many inaccuracies result in a weak analysis.

## Film studies

*Hester Street* is an important example of American independent cinema, a sector which has received scholarly interest since the 1990s. Peter Lev included *Hester Street* in his chapter on 'Feminisms' (2000), a grouping which emphasises the marginality of the film and film-maker. Emanuel Levy considered 'Female/Feminist Sensibility' in his study of American independent film, arguing that despite the low percentage of women making films professionally, '[t]he significant issue, however, is not the number of women film-makers, but the nature of their creative expression. Is there a distinctly female sensibility in indie narratives written and directed by women?' (1999: 248). We can respond to Levy's question from a feminist perspective by turning to film theorist Teresa de Lauretis, who reasoned against asking 'whether there is a feminine or female aesthetic, or a specific language of women's cinema', arguing that this is a reductive approach which supports a culture and critical framework based on work by men. Instead, de Lauretis advocated for new ways of understanding how female subjectivity is constructed and represented on screen (1990: 292). Levy criticised *Hester Street* as 'small and anecdotal', lacking 'plot or in-depth characterization' and featuring 'shallow roles', seeming to resent the focus on female characters. He also noted Mamie's 'crass gaiety – and large bosom' (1999: 352): her unremarkable bosom is in fact covered with high-necked blouses throughout the film. Levy's misjudgement of the 'significant issue' deflects from the social and industrial circumstances which were fundamental to Micklin Silver's career and the production of *Hester Street*, namely the number of women making films, which meant a lack of finance and supportive networks.

Maya Montañez Smukler's research into the production background of Joan Micklin Silver's films provides a significant contribution to current scholarship (2018, 2022). Until these publications, *Hester Street* rarely featured in major surveys of American independent film-making,[8] or was mentioned in passing.[9] Micklin Silver is overlooked or acknowledged only briefly in many recent volumes attempting to shed light on women working in film.[10] From a scholarly perspective, there has been little close analysis of *Hester Street* in the field of feminist film studies, but it has been considered primarily as a historical document that can tell us about American Jewish life in the 1890s and the struggles of new immigrants. Some universities, predominantly in the US, include *Hester Street* on curricula for courses about Jewish identity and ethnicity, the history of American immigration, New York over time, and less frequently on courses about women in film-making. Tim Lanza, film restorer and archivist who worked on the Cohen Media Group's 4K release of the film, suggested that *Hester Street* has been 'ghettoised' into Jewish studies programmes despite its sustained appeal among diverse public audiences (2024). The popularity of *Hester Street* over the past fifty years has not been reflected in its critical and academic reception. Is this due to more than simple prejudice towards Jewish women? Is it still too Jewish to be mainstream; too ethnic to be universal; too conventional a narrative to be avant-garde; too romantic to be feminist; too feminist to be Hollywood New Wave?

Naficy's definition of accented films as 'interstitial', because they are made outside mainstream film industries and social formations, helps us to understand why *Hester Street* elides straightforward classification: 'Consequently, they are simultaneously local and global, and they resonate against the prevailing cinematic production practices.' He noted how accented films both represent and shape the cultures of exile and diaspora 'by expressing, allegorizing, commenting upon, and critiquing the home and host societies and cultures and the deterritorialized conditions of the filmmakers' (2001: 4). *Hester Street*, considered in this light, is a product of the circumstances of its creation and a commentary on them. It is an American tale that comments on the difficulties of American identity, an independently produced and distributed film made by a woman, operating against the grain. *Hester Street* does not neatly fall within established genres, but it does engage with 'prevailing cinematic production practices' through elements of narrative and cinematic style. It also critiques mainstream cinematic practices through depicting Gitl as a thinking, feeling subject. *Hester Street* expresses exilic and diasporic culture through Yiddish, 'a non-territorial language' (Pasikowska-Schnass 2022: 2), and adapting its source text, *Yekl*. In *Hester Street*, Micklin Silver expresses both the tensions of the Jewish diaspora and of being an independent, female film-maker.

## *Hester Street* today

Joan Micklin Silver died on 31 December 2020, seven years after Raphael's sudden death in a skiing accident. Looking back on her life and career, several obituaries cited the comment about 'woman directors' being 'one more problem we don't need'. The repetition in the context of appraising Micklin Silver's long career enhanced her posthumous reputation as a trailblazer working against a system, and public interest in her was renewed. Her death coincided with the project to restore and re-release much of her work. During the most acute phase of the Covid-19 pandemic between 2020 and

2021, cinema attendance was reduced but online streaming increased: *Hester Street* could reach new audiences again.

The legacy of *Hester Street* is the path forged by Micklin Silver, an independent film-maker who made the film that she wanted to make, and proved wrong the naysayers who thought that a black-and-white film, in Yiddish, directed by a woman would never reach a mass audience.

Gitl's character refuses to conform to stereotype. She represents the generation of Micklin Silver's parents and grandparents who made significant geographical and psychological journeys.[11] A 1974 *Ms.* magazine article asked, 'Is It Kosher to Be Feminist?' and expressed the lack of representation which *Hester Street* would soon challenge:

In the past few years many Jewish women have come to question the ugly stereotypes foisted upon them by male Jewish literati and comedians; they have also rejected the strict sex-role division within the Jewish tradition. They are searching for testimony and their own past for the heroines ignored within Jewish culture – and finding them. Admiring the strengths of their grandmothers, they seek new ways to express their own talents.

(Hyman et al. 1974: 78)

Women then, and now, look to the past for role models, restoring respect to their overlooked or undervalued achievements.

Echoing Naficy's view that accented films are 'simultaneously local and global', Dina Micklin Silver encapsulated the intergenerational importance of *Hester Street* for her personally, and for audiences:

In crafting a story so specific to an Ashkenazi Jewish family in New York City, my mother captured the universality of the immigrant experience. One that is felt in all cultures and people around the world as they combine bravery, hard work, unbending determination and a certain amount of luck to succeed in their goals.

Joan Micklin Silver, c. 1975 (courtesy Nebraska Jewish Historical Society)

It's a story about what it means to be religious, to be a woman in America, to be in love. It is the story of the fierce protection a mother has for a child while facing the unknown. Themes that resonate with everyone – immigrant or not. (2024)

Situating *Hester Street* today means looking back to trace its own long, long journey. With *Hester Street* in the spotlight, we can recognise the achievements of Joan Micklin Silver and the continued impact of her debut feature film.

# Notes

**1** See the Tenement Museum in New York, <https://www.tenement.org> (accessed 2 September 2024).
**2** See Schreiber (2003).
**3** See Morgenstern (2024).
**4** Translation unknown. *Schnoozer* is likely not a real Yiddish word but suggests an insult towards Mamie.
**5** As praised in the 'Eishet Chayil' ('A Woman of Valour') poem, traditionally sung by husbands to their wives.

**6** For example, Mock (2007), Goldman (2013) and Ross et al. (2017).
**7** Notably Bial (2005).
**8** Absent, for example, from Tzioumakis (2006), Wood (2009), Krämer and Tzioumakis (2018).
**9** For instance, in King et al. (2018).
**10** Such as Malone (2017, 2018) and O'Hara (2021).
**11** For Jewish women's perspectives on maternal ancestry, see Antler (2007) and Stahl Weinberg (1988).

# Credits

**Hester Street**
USA
1975

**Directed by**
Joan Micklin Silver
**Produced by**
Raphael D. Silver
**Screenplay by**
Joan Micklin Silver
Based on *Yekl* by
Abraham Cahan

© 1974 Midwest Film
Productions, Inc.

**Director of Photography**
Kenneth Van Sickle
**Production Designer**
Stuart Wurtzel
**Edited by**
Katherine Wenning
**Music Adapted by**
William Bolcom
**Associate Producer**
David Appleton
**Art Director**
Edward Haynes
**Costumes**
Robert Pusilo
**Set Builder**
Joe Petruccio
**Casting**
Jay Wolf
**Dialogue Coach**
Michael Gorrin
**Sound Recordist**
William Daly
**Boom**
Peter Stein

**Gaffer**
Carl Teitelbaum
**Best Boy**
Joe Rivers
**Assistant Camera**
Jim Reilly
David Boehm
**Property Master**
Joe Petruccio
**Assistant Props**
Neal DeLuca
Taylor Pape
**Key Grip**
Sal Barone
**Script Clerk**
Sharon Sachs
**Wardrobe**
David Charles
**Hair Stylist**
Steve Atha
**Production Manager**
David Appleton
**Assistant Directors**
Jack Baran
Mik Cribben
**Production Secretary**
Deirdre Baran
**Assistant Editor**
Hal Levinsohn
**Dance Coach**
Art Ostrin
**Original Music by**
Herbert L. Clarke
**Additional Music by**
William Bolcom
**Cornet Soloist**
Gerard Schwarz
**Sound Editor**
Jack Fitzstephens

**Post-production Sound**
Image Sound Service
**Production Assistants**
Martin Nicholson
Paul Sparks
Fawn Yacker
Keith Rocke
Maris Johnson
Mary Kelly
Rick Fernicola
Julio Neri
**Rerecording Mixer**
Dick Vorisek
Processing Movielab
**Opticals**
Film Opticals, Inc.
**Titles**
QQ Titles

Special Thanks to
The Jewish Museum,
New York

**CAST**
**Steven Keats**
Jake
**Carol Kane**
Gitl
**Mel Howard**
Bernstein
**Dorrie Kavanaugh**
Mamie
**Doris Roberts**
Mrs Kavarsky
**Stephen Strimpell**
Joe Peltner
**Lauren Frost**
Fanny
**Paul Freedman**
Joey

**Martin Garner**
boss
**Leib Lensky**
peddler
**Zane Lasky**
greenhorn
**Zvee Scooler**
rabbi
**Eda Reiss Merin**
rabbi's wife
**Robert Lesser**
lawyer
**Joanna Merlin**
Jake's landlady
**Claudia Silver**
Feigie
**Edward Crowley**
inspector

**Philip Sterling**
Mr Lipman
**Sol Frieder**
scribe
**Joel Wolfe**
Kaminsky
**Mordecai Lawner**
waiter
**Lin Shaye**
whore
**Anna Berger**
poultry woman
**Bert Salzman**
Zalman

*uncredited*
**Billy Natbony**

**Production Details**
35mm
1.85:1
Black and white
Mono
Running time:
89 minutes

**Release Details**
US theatrical release
on 19 October 1975
by Midwest Films
UK theatrical release
in 1975 by Connoisseur
Film Ltd

# Bibliography

Abrams, Nathan (2012), *The New Jew in Film: Exploring Jewishness and Judaism in Contemporary Cinema* (London and New York: I. B. Tauris).

AFI (2022), 'Hester Street', American Film Institute, 2 May. Available at: <https://www.afi.com/news/hester-street-1975-afi-catalog-spotlight/> (accessed 9 August 2024).

Antler, Joyce (1995), 'Hester Street', in Ted Mico, John Miller-Monzon and David Rubel (eds), *Past Imperfect: History According to the Movies* (New York: Henry Holt and Company), pp. 187–81.

Antler, Joyce (ed.) (1998), *Talking Back: Images of Jewish Women in American Popular Culture* (Waltham, MA: Brandeis University Press).

Antler, Joyce (2007), *You Never Call! You Never Write! A History of the Jewish Mother* (New York: Oxford University Press).

Balsam, Mark (2024), Zoom interview with the author (13 August).

Barkley, Richard (1975), 'Hester Street', *Sunday Express*, 2 November, p. 22.

Baron, Lawrence (2021), 'The Pioneering American Jewish Women Directors: From Elaine May to Claudia Weill', in Leonard J. Greenspoon (ed.), *Jews and Gender* (West Lafayette, IN: Purdue University Press), pp. 217–44.

Baron, Lawrence and Liliane Targownik (2003), 'An Interview with Liliane Targownik', *Shofar* vol. 22 no. 1, pp. 117–21.

Berke, Annie (2021), 'Though It Looked to the Past, "Hester Street" Was Way Ahead of Its Time', *Forward*, 23 September. Available at: <https://forward.com/culture/475816/hester-street-restoration-cohen-media-group-joan-micklin-silver-carol-kane/> (accessed 28 February 2024).

Bial, Henry (2005), *Acting Jewish: Negotiating Ethnicity on the American Stage and Screen* (Ann Arbor: University of Michigan Press).

Bishop, Alice (2014), 'The Vintage Aesthetic: The Function of Contemporary Black & White Cinema', *The Artifice*, 25 January. Available at: <https://the-artifice.com/contemporary-black-white-cinema/> (accessed 3 May 2024).

Blacher Cohen, Sarah (ed.) (1986), *The Jewish-American Stage and Screen: From Hester Street to Hollywood* (Bloomington: Indiana University Press).

Blumenson, S. L. (1950), 'From the American Scene. Culture on Rutgers Square: The Fervent Days on East Broadway', *Commentary* vol. 10 (July), pp. 65–74. Available at: <https://www.commentary.org/articles/commentary-bk/from-the-american-scene-culture-on-rutgers-square/> (accessed 23 May 2024).

Bolton, Lucy (2011), *Film and Female Consciousness: Irigaray, Cinema and Thinking Women* (London: Palgrave Macmillan).

Brook, Vincent (2019), 'A Wave of Their Own: How Jewish Filmmakers Invented the New Hollywood', *Jewish Film & New Media* vol. 7 no. 1, pp. 48–80.

Cahan, Abraham (1896), *Yekl: A Tale of the New York Ghetto* (New York: D. Appleton and Company). Available at: <https://www.gutenberg.org/files/36715/36715-h/36715-h.htm> (accessed 28 February 2024).

Castell, David (1975), 'Hester Street', *Sunday Telegraph*, 2 November, p. 16.

Champlin, Charles (1975), 'Fiddler on Hester Street', *Los Angeles Times*, 16 May, sec. View, p. 185.

Clifford, James (1994), 'Diasporas', *Cultural Anthropology* vol. 9 no. 3, pp. 302–38.

Cohen, Robin (1997), *Global Diasporas: An Introduction* (London: University College Press).

Davies, Russell (1975), 'Hester Street', *Observer*, 2 November, p. 28.

de Lauretis, Teresa (1990), 'Rethinking Women's Cinema: Aesthetics and Feminist Theory', in Patricia Erens (ed.), *Issues in Feminist Film Criticism* (Bloomington and Indianapolis: Indiana University Press), pp. 288–308.

Deutchman, Ira (2024), Zoom interview with the author (14 August).

Diner, Hasia R. (2000), *Lower East Side Memories* (Princeton and Oxford: Princeton University Press).

Diner, Hasia R. (2011), 'The Right Film at the Right Time: Hester Street as a Reflection of its Era', in Lawrence Baron (ed.), *The Modern Jewish Experience in World Cinema* (Waltham, MA: Brandeis University Press), pp. 98–105.

Doane, Mary Ann (1991), *Femmes Fatales: Feminism, Film Theory, Psychoanalysis* (New York and London: Routledge).

Dundes, Alan (1985), 'The J. A. P. and the J. A. M. in American Jokelore', *The Journal of American Folklore* vol. 98 no. 390, pp. 456–75.

Ebiri, Bilge (2021), 'Carol Kane Looks Back on *Hester Street*, Pushing Away Fame, and Not Going to Mexico with Andy Kaufman', *Vulture*, 1 October. Available at: <https://www.vulture.com/2021/10/carol-kane-looks-back-on-hester-street-and-wicked.html> (accessed 29 August 2024).

Eder, Richard (1975), 'Pathos and Wit Light Up "Hester St."', *New York Times*, 20 October, p. 44.

Epstein, Lawrence J. (2013), *American Jewish Films: The Search for Identity* (Jefferson, NC, and London: McFarland & Company).

Erens, Patricia (1984), *The Jew in American Cinema* (Bloomington: Indiana University Press).

Erens, Patricia (ed.) (1990), *Issues in Feminist Film Criticism* (Bloomington and Indianapolis: Indiana University Press).

Erens, Patricia (2008), 'Film', in Jack Fischel (ed.), *Encyclopedia of Jewish American Popular Culture* (Westport, CT: Greenwood), pp. 124–34.

Fishman, Sylvia Barack (1998), 'I of the Beholder: Jews and Gender in Film and Popular Culture', The Hadassah Research Institute on Jewish Women, Working Paper Series, no. 1 (May) (Waltham, MA: Brandeis University Press), pp. 1–42.

Follows, Stephen (2024), 'When Did Colour Films Eclipse Black-and-white Films?', 18 March. Available at: https://stephenfollows.com/p/when-did-colour-films-eclipse-black-and-white-films (accessed 8 January 2025).

Freud, Sigmund (1955 [1919]), 'The "Uncanny"', in *The Complete Psychological Works of Sigmund Freud*, Vol. XVII, trans. Alix Strachey (London: Hogarth Press), pp. 217–57.

Friedman, Lester D. (1987), *The Jewish Image in American Film: 70 Years of Hollywood's Vision of Jewish Characters and Themes* (Secaucus, NJ: Citadel Press).

Friedman, Sharon and Stephen Steinberg (1976), 'Hester Street: The Politics of Culture', *Jump Cut* nos. 12/13 (December), pp. 33–4.

Goldman, Eric A. (2011), 'Hester Street', Library of Congress. Available at: <https://www.loc.gov/static/programs/national-film-preservation-board/documents/hester%20street.pdf> (accessed 28 February 2024).

Goldman, Eric A. (2013), *The American Jewish Story through Cinema* (Austin: University of Texas Press).

Goldsmith, Arnold L. (1979), '"A Curse on Columbus": Twentieth-Century Jewish-American Fiction and the Theme of Disillusionment', *Studies in American Jewish Literature (1975–1979)* vol. 5 no. 2, pp. 47–55.

Goodman, Walter (1975), '"Hester Street" Overpraised and Overdone', *New York Times*, 2 November, p. 151.

Gottlieb, Linda (n.d.), 'Joan Micklin Silver, 1935–2020', Jewish Women's Archive. Available at: <https://jwa.org/weremember/silver-joan> (accessed 7 August 2024).

Gregory, James (2022), 'New York Migration History 1850–2022', America's Great Migrations Project. Available at: <https://depts.washington.edu/moving1/NewYork.shtml> (accessed 24 April 2024).

Hall, Stuart (1993), 'Encoding, Decoding', in Simon During (ed.), *The Cultural Studies Reader* (London and New York: Routledge), pp. 90–103.

Hammerman, Shaina (2018), *Silver Screen, Hasidic Jews: The Story of an Image* (Bloomington: Indiana University Press).

Haskell, Molly (1975), 'How an Independent Filmmaker Beat the System (With Her Husband's Help)', *Village Voice*, 22 September, pp. 83–6.

Hoberman, J. (1995), *Bridge of Light: Yiddish Film Between Two Worlds* (Philadelphia, PA: Temple University Press).

Hyman, Paula, Audrey Gellis and Bracha Sacks (1974), 'Is It Kosher to Be Feminist?', *Ms.*, July, pp. 76–83, 108–10.

Irigaray, Luce (1985), *This Sex Which Is Not One*, trans. Catherine Porter (Ithaca, NY: Cornell University Press).

Jacobson, Matthew Frye (2006), *Roots Too: White Ethnic Revival in Post-Civil Rights America* (Cambridge, MA: Harvard University Press).

Kael, Pauline (1975), 'The Current Cinema: Becoming an American', *New Yorker* vol. 51 no. 40, pp. 167–8.

King, Geoff, Claire Molloy and Yannis Tzioumakis (eds) (2012), *American Independent Cinema: Indie, Indiewood and Beyond* (Oxford and New York: Routledge).

Krämer, Peter and Yannis Tzioumakis (2018), *The Hollywood Renaissance: Revisiting American Cinema's Most Celebrated Era* (New York: Bloomsbury Academic).

Lanza, Tim (2024), Zoom interview with the author (30 August).

Lennard, Dominic, R. Barton Palmer and Murray Pomerance (eds) (2022), *The Other Hollywood Renaissance* (Edinburgh: Edinburgh University Press).

Lev, Peter (2000), *American Films of the 70s: Conflicting Visions* (Austin: University of Texas Press).

Levy, Emanuel (1999), *Cinema of Outsiders: The Rise of American Independent Film* (New York and London: New York University Press).

Library of Congress (2011), 'National Film Registry: More Than a Box of Chocolates', 27 December. Available at: <https://www.loc.gov/item/prn-11-240/2011-national-film-registry-more-than-a-box-of-chocolates/> (accessed 7 January 2025).

Malcolm, Derek (1975), 'Hester Street', *Guardian*, 30 October, p. 8.

Malone, Alicia (2017), *Backwards and in Heels: The Past, Present and Future of Women Working in Film* (Coral Gables, FL: Mango).

Malone, Alicia (2018), *The Female Gaze: Essential Movies Made by Women* (Coral Gables, FL: Mango).

Matłoka, Magdalena (2015), 'The Everyday Life of Lower East Side Jews on the Turn of the 19th and 20th Century – Selected Aspects in the Light of American Daily Press', *Scientific Journals of the Society of Doctoral Students of the Jagiellonian University* vol. 11 no. 2, pp. 81–96. Available at: <https://doktoranci.uj.edu.pl/documents/1167150/5184220c-78bc-4761-8aee-50f6ced18239#page=81> (accessed 26 April 2024).

McBride, Joseph (1976), 'Overcome Exhibs Fear of Yiddish, 1896: "Hester Street" Strictly Uphill', *Variety*, 25 February, sec. Pictures, p. 7.

Melnikoff, Pamela (1976), 'At Last, Film Jews Are Real', *Jewish Chronicle*, 23 April, p. 10.

Meyers, Helene (2021), *Movie-Made Jews: An American Tradition* (New Brunswick, NJ: Rutgers University Press).

Michel, Sonya (1977), '"Yekl" and "Hester Street": Was Assimilation Really Good for the Jews?', *Literature/Film Quarterly* vol. 5 no. 2, pp. 142–6.

Michel, Sonya (1994), 'Jews, Gender, American Cinema', in Lynn Davidman and Shelly Tenenbaum (eds), *Feminist Perspectives on Jewish Studies* (New Haven, CT, and London: Yale University Press).

Micklin Silver, Dina (2024), 'My Mother's Classic Jewish Film "Hester Street" Deserves Its Renaissance', *Kveller*, 21 March. Available at: <https://

www.kveller.com/my-mothers-classic-jewish-film-hester-street-deserves-its-renaissance/> (accessed 9 August 2024).

Micklin Silver, Joan (1979), 'The American Film Institute Seminar with Joan Micklin Silver', 26 October, American Film Institute, Centre for Advanced Film Studies, Beverly Hills, California. Transcript pp. 1–51.

Micklin Silver, Joan (1991), 'Harold Lloyd Master Seminar', American Film Institute, Centre for Advanced Film and Television Studies, Los Angeles, California, 23 October. Transcript pp. 1–47.

Micklin Silver, Joan (2005), 'Visual History with Joan Micklin Silver', Interview by Michael Pressman, Directors Guild of America. Available at: <https://www.dga.org/Craft/VisualHistory/Interviews/Joan-Micklin-Silver.aspx> (accessed 29 February 2024).

Micklin Silver, Joan (2006), 'NYWIFT Archive Interview with Joan Micklin Silver', Interview by Norma Davidoff, New York Women in Film & Television. Available at: <https://www.youtube.com/watch?v=ZYFKZK7svpY> (accessed 19 November 2024).

Micklin Silver, Joan (2021 [2017]), 'Conversations from the Quad', Interview by Shonni Enelow, Hester Street DVD, Cohen Film Collection.

Micklin Silver, Joan and Raphael Silver (1975), 'Explorations: On "Hester Street"', American Film vol. 1 no. 1 (October), pp. 78–80.

Micklin Silver, Joan and Raphael Silver, (2021 [2004]), Audio commentary, Hester Street DVD, Cohen Film Collection.

Mock, Roberta (2007), Jewish Women on Stage, Film, and Television (New York: Palgrave Macmillan).

Montañez Smukler, Maya (2018), Liberating Hollywood: Women Directors and the Feminist Reform of 1970s American Cinema (New Brunswick, NJ: Rutgers University Press).

Montañez Smukler, Maya (2022), 'New Hollywood Crossover: Joan Micklin Silver and the Indie-Studio Divide', in Dominic Lennard, R. Barton Palmer and Murray Pomerance (eds), The Other Hollywood Renaissance (Edinburgh: Edinburgh University Press), pp. 222–35.

Morgenstern, Michael (2024), 'The Forward: A Gallery of Missing Husbands (1908–1920), JewishGen, The Genealogical Research Division of Museum of Jewish Heritage. Available at: <https://www.jewishgen.org/databases/usa/missinghusbands.html> (accessed 9 July 2024).

Morris Purdee, Roberta (2024), Zoom interview with the author (25 March).

Naficy, Hamid (2001), An Accented Cinema: Exilic and Diasporic Filmmaking (Princeton, NJ: Princeton University Press).

New-York Tribune (1901), 'New-York Pedlers', 11 August, sec. Illustrated Supplement, p. 8.

O'Hara, Helen (2021), Women Vs Hollywood: The Fall and Rise of Women in Film (London: Robinson).

Pally, Marcia (1984), 'Kaddish: For the Fading Image of Jews in Film', *Film Comment* vol. 20 no. 1, pp. 49–55.

Pasikowska-Schnass, Magdalena (2022), 'Yiddish Language and Culture and its Post-Holocaust Fate in Europe', European Parliamentary Research Service, European Parliament. Available at: <https://www.europarl.europa.eu/RegData/etudes/BRIE/2022/698881/EPRS_BRI(2022)698881_EN.pdf> (accessed 29 February 2024).

Polland, Annie and Daniel Soyer (2012), *Emerging Metropolis: New York Jews in the Age of Immigration, 1840–1920* (New York and London: New York University Press).

Polonsky, Antony (2010), *The Jews in Poland and Russia*, Vol. II: 1881–1914 (Liverpool: Liverpool University Press).

Popkin, Henry (1952), 'The Vanishing Jew of Our Popular Culture: The Little Man Who is No Longer There', *Commentary* no. 14 (July), pp. 46–55. Available at: <https://www.commentary.org/articles/henry-popkin/the-vanishing-jew-of-our-popular-culturethe-little-man-who-is-no-longer-there/> (accessed 26 March 2024).

Prell, Riv-Ellen (1998), 'Cinderellas Who (Almost) Never Become Princesses: Subversive Representations of Jewish Women in Postwar Popular Novels', in Joyce Antler (ed.), *Talking Back: Images of Jewish Women in American Popular Culture* (Waltham, MA: Brandeis University Press), pp. 123–38.

Prell, Riv-Ellen (1999), *Fighting to Become Americans: Jews, Gender, and the Anxiety of Assimilation* (Boston, MA: Beacon Press).

Pucker Rivo, Sharon (1998), 'Projected Images: Portraits of Jewish Women in Early American Film', in Joyce Antler (ed.), *Talking Back: Images of Jewish Women in American Popular Culture* (Waltham, MA: Brandeis University Press), pp. 30–49.

Reed-Wood, Louis (2022), 'Hester Street with Miriam Borden', Off-Campus History, 10 October. Available at: <https://podcasts.apple.com/gb/podcast/off-campus-history/id1574056925?i=1000582127014> (accessed 19 July 2024).

Rich, B. Ruby (1998), *Chick Flicks: Theories and Memories of the Feminist Film Movement* (Durham, NC, and London: Duke University Press).

Rosen, Marjorie (1975), 'Three Films in Search of a Distributor', *Ms.*, July, pp. 30–3.

Rosenberg, Joel (1996), 'Jewish Experience on Film – An American Overview', *American Jewish Year Book* vol. 96, pp. 3–50.

Ross, Steven J., Michael Renov, Vincent Brook and Lisa Ansell (eds) (2017), *From Shtetl to Stardom: Jews and Hollywood* (West Lafayette, IN: Purdue University Press).

Rubinow, Isaac Max (1959 [1902–3]), 'The Jewish Question in New York City', trans. Leo Shpall, *Publications of the American Jewish Historical Society* vol. 49 no. 2, pp. 90–136.

Ryzik, Melena (2024), 'The Highly Deceptive, Deeply Loved, Down-to-

Earth Carol Kane', *New York Times*, 29 August. Available at: <https://www.nytimes.com/2024/08/29/movies/carol-kane-princess-bride-between-the-temples.html#> (accessed 30 August 2024).

Safran, William (1991), 'Diasporas in Modern Societies: Myths of Homeland and Return', *Diaspora: A Journal of Transnational Studies* vol. 1 no. 1, pp. 83–99.

Schreiber, Lynne (ed.) (2003), *Hide and Seek: Jewish Women and Hair Covering* (New York and Jerusalem: Urim Publications).

Shepard, Richard F. (1975), 'A Generation Returns to Hester St., Where It All Began', *New York Times*, 11 November, p. 66.

Shorter, Eric (1975), 'Hester Street', *Daily Telegraph*, 31 October, p. 13.

Silver, Raphael (2021 [2004]), Interview, *Hester Street* DVD, Cohen Film Collection.

Singer, Isaac Bashevis (1989 [1943]), 'Problems of Yiddish Prose in America', trans. Robert H. Wolf, *Prooftexts* vol. 9 no. 1, pp. 5–12.

Stahl Weinberg, Sydney (1988), *The World of Our Mothers: The Lives of Jewish Immigrant Women* (New York: Schocken Books).

Stanislawski, Michael (1988), *For Whom Do I Toil? Judah Leib Gordon and the Crisis of Russian Jewry* (New York and Oxford: Oxford University Press).

Steinmetz, Sol (2001), *Yiddish and English: The Story of Yiddish in America*, 2nd edn (Tuscaloosa: University of Alabama Press).

Thirkell, Arthur (1975), 'Tailor Beware!', *Daily Mirror*, 31 October, p. 23.

Tzioumakis, Yannis (2006), *American Independent Cinema: An Introduction* (Edinburgh: Edinburgh University Press).

Vardoulakis, Dimitris (2006), 'The Return of Negation: The Doppelgänger in Freud's "The Uncanny"', *SubStance* vol. 35 no. 2, pp. 100–16.

Wagner, Julia (2022), 'Bar Mitzvah Boy', Booklet, *Play for Today: Volume 3* Blu-ray box set (London: BFI), pp. 19–24.

Whitfield, Stephen J. (2019), 'Adaptation and Autonomy on the Lower East Side: The Jews of *Hester Street*', in Matthew Christopher Hulbert and John C. Inscoe (eds), *Writing History with Lightning: Cinematic Representations of Nineteenth-Century America* (Baton Rouge: Louisiana State University Press), pp. 289–99.

Wood, Jason (2009), *100 American Independent Films*, 2nd edn (London: BFI/Palgrave).

Wurtzel, Stuart (2024), Zoom interview with the author (13 March).

YIVO (2014), 'Basic Facts about Yiddish', YIVO Institute for Jewish Research. Available at: <https://www.yivo.org/cimages/basic_facts_about_yiddish_2014.pdf> (accessed 18 December 2024).